# po'boy

**LOUISIANA TRUE** books tell the stories of the state's iconic places, traditions, foods, and objects. Each book centers on one element of Louisiana's culture, unpacking the myths, misconceptions, and historical realities behind everything that makes our state unique, from above-ground cemeteries to zydeco.

---

# po'boy

## BURKE BISCHOFF

Louisiana State University Press

Baton Rouge

Published by Louisiana State University Press

lsupress.org

LSU Press Paperback Original

Manufactured in the United States of America

First printing

Designer: Barbara Neely Bourgoyne

Typeface: Source Sans Variable

Printer and binder: Integrated Books International (IBI)

All photographs are reproduced courtesy of the author.

Library of Congress Cataloging-in-Publication Data

Names: Bischoff, Burke, author.

Title: Po'boy / Burke Bischoff.

Description: Baton Rouge : Louisiana State University Press, [2023] |
   Series: Louisiana true | Includes bibliographical references.

Identifiers: LCCN 2023012913 (print) | LCCN 2023012914 (ebook) | ISBN 978-0-8071-8047-1
   (paperback) | ISBN 978-0-8071-8120-1 (pdf) | ISBN 978-0-8071-8119-5 (epub)

Subjects: LCSH: Sandwiches—Louisiana—New Orleans—History. | Cooking, American—
   Louisiana style.

Classification: LCC TX818 .B525 2023 (print) | LCC TX818 (ebook) | DDC
   641.8409763/35—dc23/eng/20230406

LC record available at https://lccn.loc.gov/2023012913

LC ebook record available at https://lccn.loc.gov/2023012914

Thank you to Sandy Whann, Joanne and Ken Domilise, Linh Tran Garza, Justin Kennedy, Jason Gendusa, Jane Wolfe, Eric Baucom, and Russell Hendrick.

Your knowledge is immense and my gratitude is deep.

# contents

# po'boy

Hot sausage patty po'boy from Melba's.

# 1

# Introduction to an Icon
## *What Exactly Is a Po'Boy?*

New Orleans, the most populated city in the state of Louisiana, is a true gem in the United States of America. Founded in 1718 by Jean-Baptiste Le Moyne de Bienville and made into the territorial capital of the immense French Louisiana colony in 1722, the Crescent City has been able to set itself apart from larger American cities by holding on to its deeply seated French heritage while also incorporating elements from multiple other sources throughout the course of its more than three hundred years of history. Its time as the capital of Spanish Louisiana from 1769 to 1801, its transfer to the United States from France during the Louisiana Purchase in 1803, and its diverse population with ancestral roots in France, West Africa, Spain, Haiti, Germany, Sicily, Ireland, Latin America, Vietnam, and many other places have all contributed to a cultural legacy that can only be found in New Orleans.

This multilingual history and mix of cultures has not only elevated New Orleans's status as one of the most unusual cities in America, but also made it one of the most recognizable cities in the world. Its status in popular culture has been cemented by its numerous appearances in movies, music, books, and other forms of art. The Big Easy may be known best for its contributions to jazz music, but it has also been home to important musicians in other popular musical genres, such as rock and roll, rhythm and blues, and hip-hop. New Orleans Mardi Gras is one of the most iconic Carnival celebrations in the world, standing alongside the revelries found in Venice, Nice, and Rio de Janeiro. But perhaps the best representation of NOLA's distinctive cultural identity is its food.

Traditional New Orleans cuisine is made up of dishes that have been specifically created in the city, while also incorporating food that developed in the surrounding areas of southern Louisiana and the Mississippi River Delta. Thus, its main influences include Creole cuisine (which was developed from all of the different ethnic groups present in the colony before the Louisiana Purchase), Cajun cuisine (which came from the Acadians who settled in Louisiana after being deported from their homeland in Canada during the French and Indian War), and soul food (cuisine with West African and Native American influences, developed by African Americans living in the Deep South). Dishes like gumbo, jambalaya, étouffée, chargrilled oysters, red beans and rice, turtle soup, beignets, and so much more are synonymous with the City That Care Forgot and are recognizable around the world. It also helps that most people in the city, from the most celebrated chefs to people just fixing food for their neighbors, know how to cook.

"There's a longstanding culinary tradition here where everyone in the family is growing up in part of the kitchen," Eric Baucom, chef, owner, and operator of Killer PoBoys, says.

Perhaps one of the simplest, and most popular, dishes to be birthed in New Orleans is the humble po'boy sandwich. Po'boys (also spelled "po-boys" and "poboys" depending on personal preference as there really is no common consensus) can be found all over Louisiana and the Gulf South. In fact, whenever there is a "New Orleans–themed" restaurant, whether it be in or out of Louisiana, there's a good chance that po'boys will be on its menu.

For a city that's known for its creative food and cocktails, why would a sandwich be so beloved? What exactly is a "po'boy" and how does it represent an entire city along with gumbo and Mardi Gras? How long has it been in the Big Easy? What sets it apart from the multitude of other classic sandwiches like Reubens, clubs, and croque monsieurs? And, most importantly of all, why is it so delicious?

First things first: "po'boy" is New Orleans slang for "poor boy."

"We call it 'po'boys,'" Joanne Domilise, general manager of Domilise's Po-Boy & Bar, says. "That was something that started as 'poor boys' and, through the years, many restaurants have just simplified it, made it faster. 'Po'boys' instead of 'poor boys.'"

"If you look on any old wording about that sandwich, it wasn't 'p-o-apostrophe,'" Justin Kennedy, general manager of Parkway Bakery & Tavern, explains. "It was 'p-o-o-r b-o-y' . . . I don't expect people to pronounce it that way because, especially New Orleans people, their accent doesn't go that way. We don't go 'poor.' We go 'po.' Just like when people say, 'Where y'at?' You know, 'Where are you at?' We like to shorten things up a little bit. I say 'po'boy' all day long, but if I were to spell it out, it's definitely 'p-o-o-r b-o-y.'"

While the shortened version is the most popular and recognizable way to refer to the dish, there are still plenty of locals who find themselves using the original pronunciation of "poor boys." Some even go back and forth between the two names because, just like how there is no consensus on how to spell "po'boy," either pronunciation is valid in its own way.

"I'm guilty of both," Jason Gendusa, baker and owner of John Gendusa Bakery, says. "I do mostly say 'poor boy' 'cause that is the correct saying. But as we do in New Orleans, we shorten things. As long as it tastes good, you can't go wrong with what you're calling it."

"I refer to it both ways," president and owner of Leidenheimer Baking Company Sandy Whann says. "Tom Fitzmorris never approved of the shorter version, but it's unavoidable. The New Orleans vernacular almost demands it."

The shortening of "poor boy" to "po'boy" stems from the unique New Orleans dialect that is called "Yat," which takes its name from a common New Orleans phrase "Where y'at?" This vernacular is one of many that have developed in the city and is unlike any other accent found in the Deep South. Instead of sounding characteristically "southern," the accent has a lot of similarities to what is heard in New York City.

"While I was in the Navy, just meeting people, fellow Navy guys, 'Where you from? New York?'" Russell Hendrick, president and owner of Short Stop Poboys, details. "'Actually, I'm from New Orleans.' 'They don't talk like that down there.' I said, 'Well, yeah we do.'"

"I can verify that," Ken Domilise, co-owner of Domilise's Po-Boy & Bar, says. "In my career in the insurance industry, I did a lot of work with New Yorkers because we dealt with the companies, and so many people I dealt with thought I was from New York or the Bronx."

Many theories as to why a lot of New Orleanians sound like this mostly stem from New Orleans being a port city, thus giving it access to many different groups of people from both inside and outside of the United States.

"It appears like people in harbor towns, no matter where they at, they have their own little accent," Kennedy says. "If you go 45 minutes north, it's a whole different world in Louisiana, you know? It's just like New Orleans is its own little nook."

"I think the essence of why we speak the way we do is because New York and New Orleans were port cities talking together all the time," Jane Wolfe, founder and co-owner of Melba's, says. "It's all about trade, and there were no bigger ports in the United States than New York and New Orleans. And these New Yorkers were down with us and we were talking with them."

"I think it's just the difference in ethnicity in the city, really," Hendrick says. "Even if you travel around in the city, you're going to get some different Yat accents within the city."

No matter how it is pronounced, a po'boy is essentially a submarine-like sandwich. Pretty simple and to the point. However, there are different specific details that make this NOLA sandwich one of a kind. Perhaps the most important element that truly defines a po'boy is the "French bread" that holds the entire thing together. French bread, as made obvious by the name, is based on the traditional baguette that the French introduced to the region during colonial times. This type of bread is unique to the New Orleans area and will be expounded upon in a later chapter, but it's very important to know that a po'boy would completely lose its identity if this bread is substituted for anything else.

As long as French bread is included into the mix, a po'boy can contain any kind of desired contents and still be considered a true po'boy. All meat, all veggies, or a mixture of everything? It does not really matter. It's still a po'boy.

"I've eaten red beans and rice po'boys," Hendrick says. "So it can be anything. Anything that you would normally eat a piece of bread with you could actually just put in between that bread and eat it."

That may seem incredibly vague, as well as dauting, for a po'boy virgin who's looking to decide on what sandwich to try. Yes, there are almost countless different po'boys to choose from depending on the establishment, but there are some po'boys that are considered "classics" and can be regularly found in many New Orleans restaurants.

Given the city's location on the Mississippi River with access to the Gulf of Mexico, seafood is in plentiful supply and is always a favorite for any meal in any way, shape, or form. The seafood in po'boys is almost always deep fried, adding extra flavor and texture to the sandwich. Some of the most popular seafood options that are typically used include shrimp, oyster, and fish (usually catfish, but it really depends on the restaurant), while critters like crawfish, soft-shell crab, and alligator (which can either be fried or made into a sausage) are also enjoyed when these items come into season.

In addition to the plentiful amount of seafood on offer around the city, one can also find plenty of po'boys with classic sandwich fillings such as sliced ham, grilled chicken, sliced turkey, and hamburger patties. However, for more NOLA-centric options that are almost always found on menus across the city, be on the lookout for two specific types of po'boys. One is the roast beef po'boy. Napkins are highly recommended because this sandwich is almost always completely drenched in gravy, and the beef is cooked down so much it falls apart by the strand. Local New Orleanians actually have a term for that loose, tender beef with gravy: "debris."

"Debris is like a beef roast that you basically just cook down until it falls apart," Baucom says. "So it's not sliced or anything like that. It's just loose strands of meat that are falling apart from being cooked until they're that tender."

The other classic meat po'boy New Orleanians enjoy is the hot sausage po'boy. Said sausage is made with a mixture of different spices to give it a characteristic "Louisiana heat" flavor. One of the most common and popular hot sausage meats that is used by restaurants in Greater New Orleans is supplied by Patton's Sausage Company, which has its headquarters in Bogalusa, Louisiana. In addition to regular sausage links, Patton's also offers unique hot sausage patties, which are more often than not what most hot sausage po'boys are filled with.

"It's just absolutely delicious," Kennedy says. "Throw some American cheese on it, a little mayo, and yellow mustard. Knock the tongue out your mouth."

Another classic New Orleans po'boy that is a little bit harder to find is kind of an oddity at first glance: the French fry po'boy. Mostly found at the older po'boy shops in NOLA, it is exactly what it sounds like and usually comes topped with roast beef gravy. While the sandwich seems very basic and unassuming, it is actually considered by a number of locals to be one of the very first po'boys that was served in the city.

"It makes a great po'boy," Hendrick says. "French fries, a little bit of roast beef gravy on it. Like meat and potatoes on bread."

While the French bread and the fillings are the main components of any po'boy, just like any sandwich, toppings can help elevate the taste in interesting ways. For anyone looking to come to New Orleans to experience a po'boy firsthand, there is a certain term that is native to the city and must be learned in order to properly order a po'boy. The term is "dressed," as in, "Would ya like that dressed?"

"If they're ordering, we say, 'You want it dressed?'" Kennedy says. "For the tourists, we have a big sign right above the order window, about two-foot-tall, seven-foot-wide, that says, 'Dressed: lettuce, tomato, mayo, pickle.' Because people from out of town, they don't know what that means."

"What 'dressed' means is what you're going to put on it in addition to the main protein . . . dressing is specific to a restaurant," Joanne Domilise says. "My dressings are not the same as another restaurant's dressings, so it's not one thing. You need to know when you go to a restaurant, when they say 'dressed,' what is the dressing. And that's really important because customers want to say, 'Oh yeah, I want it fully dressed.' But then you'll say what the dressings are and maybe they'll say, 'Oh no, I didn't know it included pickles, and I don't like pickles.' So it depends on where you are."

There are a number of different po'boy varieties that can be found all over New Orleans, and each of the city's distinctive neighborhoods has certain po'boy shops that locals flock to. In fact, each and every local has a particular version of the sandwich that they gravitate toward.

"I am always a fan of the shrimp po'boy," Linh Tran Garza, president of Dong Phuong Baking Company, says. "Pretty simple. Shrimp po'boy, dressed, lots of mayo. Sometimes I dabble into the shrimp and oyster po'boys if I'm feeling kind of in the mood."

"Well, when it comes to seafood, it's definitely fried oyster," Whann says. "And I'm pretty basic on the others. Definitely hot roast beef. I like Swiss with mine, but I am not a lettuce and tomato guy. I'm not a 'dressed' po'boy guy, oddly enough."

"Personally, I like the simple stuff," Wolfe says. "A hot sausage, shrimp, roast beef, or a ham and cheese po'boy."

"I would say oyster," Kennedy says. "I don't eat them all the time, but those are the ones I get a craving for."

"I love seafood, so it would be a shrimp or an oyster," Hendrick says. "Maybe even a soft-shell crab. I'm kinda stuck on my own roast beef."

"My favorite po'boy is going to come from one of the old shops . . . fried shrimp, dressed, no tomato, extra mayo," Baucom says.

"Mine is fried shrimp, although that roast beef and Swiss is a very close second, and I love the hot smoke sausage," Joanne Domilise says. "Fully dressed. Everything I do is fully dressed."

"You can't go wrong with a shrimp po'boy," Gendusa says. "I think most people would say that. On the flipside, I do like a grilled chicken po'boy. They make 'em out at Parran's. Man, it just melts in your mouth. That's a little off the beaten path. If you got the right bread, I'll eat any kind of po'boy."

While the classic options are always easy and delicious choices to make when looking for great-tasting po'boys in the city, New Orleans is not known for just staying "standard." The Big Easy is a colorful city that has a passionate desire for enjoying life, and that fervent spirit consistently makes it into the way people prepare their food. Creativity is the spice of life, and New Orleans loves its spice. So while the classic po'boys are always great, trying something different and being pleasantly surprised by a creative spin on something familiar, especially from restaurants that are not exclusively tailored to just po'boys, is just as exciting.

"I mean you can go to Pascal's Manale, for instance, which no one considers to be a po'boy shop, and yet they have the BBQ shrimp po'boy," Whann says. "They invented it. Despite the fact po'boys aren't the primary on their menu, they're still serving one of the most memorable sandwiches, one of the most memorable po'boys, in the city."

New Orleanians love po'boys so much that, since 2007, large crowds celebrate the sandwich each year at the city's popular Oak Street Po'Boy Festival, which is a major food event and usually features a po'boy competition with between forty to sixty local restaurants taking part. A lot of the restaurants that attend the festival are not even po'boy shops, like Ye Olde College Inn Restaurant & Bar, which actually won "Best of Show" at the very first Oak Street Po'Boy Festival for its fried-green-tomato shrimp remoulade po'boy.

Fried-green-tomato shrimp remoulade po'boy from Ye Olde College Inn.

"Most of the restaurants that come into that festival are not even in the po'boy business," Kennedy says. "They're still restaurants, but they come do their best take on the po'boy. And to go out to that festival and win, you can't just do a shrimp or a roast beef. You got to do something different. You got to do something you can never get."

So what exactly are po'boys? Po'boys are the people's food, and the best way to connect with new people and experience anyplace for the first time is to eat what the locals eat. So, no matter if someone is trying a traditional po'boy or one of the newer spins on the sandwich, he or she will be taking part in a time-honored tradition that has been a staple in NOLA for many, many years.

"It's impossible to experience New Orleans without experiencing its food," Whann says. "We are blessed to have the Gulf [of Mexico] and to have so many incredible sources of food surrounding us. The po'boy, particularly our French bread, is really just a blank canvas for that. And the creativity of our chefs—our po'boy shops, restaurants, whatever it happens to be—I think with their creativity and the bounties of the Gulf surrounding us, I absolutely think po'boys are a true representation of the city of New Orleans. I think they have been since the early 1900s and I think they'll continue to be. They can be very upscale and they can be very down-market. They're all delicious. That's what makes them so special."

"It's definitely found itself a good home," Gendusa says. "I don't know if it would work as well anywhere else 'cause you've got to have the seafood and all that. You don't have that all over the country. We're a very good spot for all that we do."

"Po'boys are one of the real iconic dishes," Baucom says. "Everybody recognizes one. Like when you see a picture of a shrimp po'boy on TV, you know exactly where that came from. It's the people's food. It's something that you can unwarp and eat over a garbage can on the street with all your buddies while drinking a beer. It's what we're about down here. It really encapsulates the whole vibe of New Orleans in one sandwich."

"It's like walking your dog or going to church on Sunday morning," Kennedy says. "People gotta do it. They got to have their po'boy sandwich."

French fry po'boy from Parkway Bakery & Tavern.

# 2

# The Birth of a Classic
## *"Here Comes Another Poor Boy!"*

In a city as storied as New Orleans, it should come as no surprise that a multitude of interesting characters have walked its streets during its more than three hundred years of existence. Not a lot of other cities can say that they have had a French pirate help defend them during the Battle of 1812, a hairdresser who was a voodoo queen and a respected member of the community, and a nineteenth-century baroness who was shot four times in the chest at point-blank range by her father-in-law and proceeded to live for another forty years. From musicians, writers, athletes, chefs, and more, New Orleanians have made significant contributions to history and the world at large. In regard to the po'boy, no two individuals are more important to the entire history of the sandwich than the Martin brothers.

The brothers, named Bennie and Clovis Martin, are largely credited as being the originators of the modern-day New Orleans "poor boy" sandwich. Ask the many different po'boy shops in the city and, more often than not, they will chronicle the same story of the Martin brothers and what they did for members of their community that forever ties them to the history of po'boys. Many different New Orleans and national websites tell the story of the Martins, but the story is detailed quite nicely on Parkway Bakery & Tavern's website.

According to the story on the site, which was documented by the late New Orleans historian Michael Mizell-Nelson, the Martin brothers originally lived in Raceland, which is located in Lafourche Parish and part of the larger Acadiana, or "Cajun Country," region of Louisiana, until moving to New Orleans in the mid-1910s. When the brothers got to New Orleans, they first worked as streetcar conductors before deciding to open up their own eating establishment in 1922. It was called Martin Brothers' Coffee Stand & Restaurant, and it was located at the corner of North Peters Street and Ursulines Avenue in the famous French Market, which has been a fixture in the city since 1791.

The most important year for both the Martin brothers and modern po'boys was 1929, which was the start of the Great Depression. Before the widespread use of automobiles, New Orleans's streetcars (also known as trolleys in other parts of the United States) were a major lifeline for the city and its residents. Union members of the Amalgamated Association of Electric Street Railway Employees, Division 194, went on strike after negotiations for better pay were not being fulfilled. This strike caused over a thousand streetcar workers associated with the union to become unemployed. Sympathetic to their fellow streetcar comrades, the Martin brothers decided they were going to help the men affected by the strike.

"I'm looking at my bookshelf and a framed copy of a letter that they sent to the striking railcar workers, inviting these striking car men of Division 194," Leidenheimer Baking Company's president Sandy Whann says. "This is August 6th, 1929, and Clovis and Bennie Martin told members of Division 194 that 'we are with you heart and soul. And any time you are around the French Market, don't forget to drop in at Martin's Coffee Stand & Restaurant, corner of Ursuline and North Peters. Your meal is free to any members of Division 194.' And they say, 'We are with you till hell freezes, and when it does, we will furnish the blankets to keep you warm.' So, very dramatic. Of course, the striking railcar workers took them up on that offer of free food."

As the story goes, when the streetcar workers came to Martin Brothers' Coffee Stand & Restaurant, either Bennie or Clovis would shout out, "Here comes another poor boy!" and the brothers would give the workers free sandwiches during the strike. However, according to John Gendusa Bakery's owner, Jason Gendusa, the bread the Martins originally used at the beginning of the strike looked different from the modern French bread used for today's po'boys. When the brothers would cut up a French bread loaf, people would get an inconsistently sized sandwich.

"It was fat in the middle, skinny on the ends," Gendusa says. "Almost like an elongated football, to give you an idea, and they would make sandwiches on that. If you and me went to eat lunch together, and I got the middle part that was nice and wide and you got the end part, our sandwiches looked a little different."

Gendusa says the Martin brothers, looking for a way to feed the workers that came to their stand in equal amounts, approached his great-grandfather, John Gendusa, to figure out what to do.

"In '29 when the streetcar strike happened and the Martin brothers began to feed all of the streetcar workers for free, they came to my great-grandfather and were like, 'We need to find a solution to this problem,'" Gendusa explains. "Growing up in Sicily with bakeries everywhere you turn, he's like, 'Well over there, they've got this long, beautiful, uniform loaf of bread.' He's like, 'If I can do that, everyone gets the same sized sandwich.' Not sure how long it took him to get it, but he did. The 36-inch-long, uniform po'boy."

One problem with the specific details involved in the Martin brothers' story is that it happened almost one hundred years ago and the major players involved within said tale have long since passed away. As a result, while Gendusa, as well as Parkway Bakery's general manager, Justin Kennedy, says the uniform French bread that was developed by John Gendusa was 36 inches long, other sources give different numbers for how long the loaf was. Both the "History of the Poor Boy" on Parkway's website and ForknPlate's "The Po' Boy: New Orleans' Super Star Sandwich," written by Susan Waggoner, state that the loaf created in 1929 was 32 inches long, while other sources, like *64 Parishes*'s "Po-Boy Sandwich," written by Michael Mizell-Nelson, say the loaf was 40 inches long. Regardless of exactly how long the French bread loaf was, the important thing is that John Gendusa was able to develop a uniform, rectangularly shaped French bread that the Martin brothers were able to cut into even amounts to feed New Orleans's striking streetcar workers.

Another topic of speculation is what exactly the sandwiches were filled with. Again, since the streetcar strike happened so long ago, specific details are hard to come by. Some New Orleanians like Gendusa and Kennedy say the original po'boys the Martin brothers served might have been the French fry po'boy: fried potatoes drizzled with roast beef gravy or debris. Others, like Short Stop Poboys owner Russell Hendrick, say it might have been cold-cut po'boys like sliced ham, turkey, and bologna that were served. However, it can be generally agreed that the Martin brothers used fillings that were cheap and easy to quickly make for the many streetcar workers who came to their stand.

While the Martin brothers originally started to give away free sandwiches to struggling streetcar workers, the po'boy became increasingly popular with New Orleanians in general as the Great Depression dragged on into the 1930s. This was due to po'boys being both filling and cheap, which was perfect for people who were struggling to make ends meet at that time. According to Parkway's website, prices for po'boy sandwiches in the 1930s included 10 cents for a 15-inch sandwich and 15 cents for a 20-inch. From the 1930s onward, more and more shops and groceries serving "poor boy" sandwiches were appearing in New Orleans due to the recognition the Martin brothers were getting. All of the business the Martin brothers received allowed them to open even more restaurants around the city. The very last restaurant related to the Martin brothers, according to Parkway's website, was located on St. Claude Avenue until it closed down in the 1970s. As of 2022, the corner of Ursulines and North Peters, the

Corner of North Peters and Ursulines in the French Quarter.

site of the original Martin Brothers' Coffee Stand & Restaurant, is home to a number of shops selling items like hats, bags, and dresses on one side and the entrance to the open-air vendor portion of the French Market on the other side.

The story of the Martin brothers giving away free food to struggling streetcar workers has been widely accepted as the origin of the "poor boy" sandwiches, at least by most New Orleanians. However, there is another type of sandwich that not only seems a little bit similar to a po'boy, but also supposedly predates the streetcar strike and the Martin brothers' restaurant. That sandwich is called an oyster loaf. According to Roger M. Grace in an article for the *Los Angeles Metropolitan News-Enterprise,* the loaves were also called "peacemakers," on account of men apparently bringing their wives or girlfriends an oyster loaf to get back into their good graces when they came home late.

If one is going by the loosest definition of what a sandwich can be, that is, a protein or a filling surrounded by bread, then the oyster loaf definitely predates the 1929 streetcar strike both in New Orleans and on the Gulf Coast. Both *The Picayune Creole Cook Book* from New Orleans and the *Gulf City Cook Book* from Mobile, Alabama, which were published in 1901 and 1878 respectively, make mention of oyster loaves. Both recipes involve loaves of bread being stuffed with oysters. However, the recipes have slight differences from each other. *The Picayune Creole Cook Book,* which also labels oyster loaves as "la médiatirce," details that the tops of French loaves are cut off, the inside breadcrumbs are scooped out so that either creamed or broiled oysters can be placed inside, and then the top lids of the cut bread are placed back on top. While the recipe in the *Gulf City Cook Book* also involves oyster-stuffed bread loaves, noticeable differences include baker's bread being used instead of French loaves, one of the ends being cut off the bread instead of the top, and fried oysters with pickles being stuffed inside the loaf.

For an even older example, the dish is also mentioned in an 1824 cookbook by Mary Randolph entitled *The Virginia House-Wife; Or, Methodical Cook,* which is one of the earliest known American cookbooks. In the recipe that Randolph details, loaves of bread have their tops cut off and the inside crumbs scooped out and stewed in a mixture of oysters, water, and butter, which is then placed back inside the loaf.

Even though the oyster loaf clearly dates far before the Martin brothers' po'boy story, the dish has enough differences from the po'boy that it could be considered a completely separate entity. The main difference is the bread and how it is treated in both dishes. While a po'boy's French bread is cut down the middle from one side so that fillings can be placed inside, the oyster loaves have their tops cut off and are treated like a box for their oyster fillings. Also, the breads used for the oyster loaves are not consistent between the recipes. Another difference is that, while oyster loaves can call for oysters prepared in different fashions, the oysters used for oyster po'boys are almost always fried and can come with different dressings.

"My sense is that those were probably similar to what we now know as a boat loaf," Sandy Whann says. "They were very popular, particularly out by the Lake [Pontchartrain], I don't remember for how long, but definitely in the '50s and '60s. And these boat loaves were basically white bread, Pullman loaves, like you use for sliced bread. It would be unsliced and they cut the top off, hollow it out, and put a stick of butter in there, roll it around, and then filled it with fried oysters and fried shrimp. We make them, there're still customers that serve them. Obviously, the oyster loaf was not being made on what we would call a modern-day po'boy loaf. But there are certainly stories out there suggesting that other people were making sandwiches on French bread. I mean that is a plausible idea, right? But I think the sandwich will forever be connected with this railcar workers' strike in New Orleans. That's just the way history goes."

Another big difference is the level of exposure between the two dishes. Po'boys can be found all over New Orleans and surrounding parishes, with numbers upon numbers of different restaurants either featuring the sandwich on their menus or being solely dedicated to just serving po'boys. Unfortunately, not a lot of NOLA restaurants feature either oyster loaves or peacemakers, and when they do, each instance is somewhat different from the recipes that were around in the nineteenth and early twentieth centuries.

One of the city's most popular establishments, Casamento's Restaurant, which was established in 1919 and is wildly celebrated for its seafood, does have oyster loaves listed on its menu. However, Casamento's loaves utilize sliced pan bread for their fried oysters instead of traditional bread loaves or French bread. Mahony's, which has locations in both the French Quarter and Uptown New Orleans, has a peacemaker po'boy, which actually won an award at the Oak Street Po'Boy Festival according to the restaurant's website, but it contains shrimp, candied bacon, and cheddar along with fried oysters. Acme Oyster House, which has three locations in Louisiana and three others across the South, has a peacemaker po'boy that includes fried oysters and fried shrimp with Tabasco sauce. Both Bevi Seafood Company in Mid-City New Orleans and Bon Temps Boulet's Seafood Company in Metairie also list peacemakers within their menus, but as po'boys containing shrimp and roast beef debris instead of oysters.

So, while oyster loaves are older than po'boys, and there most likely have been other instances of people stuffing traditional French bread and baguettes with some kind of filling, the concept of what is a modern po'boy is firmly attributed to the Martin brothers giving free sandwiches to out-of-work streetcar employees, as well as John Gendusa developing a long, uniform French bread loaf so that all of those poor boys were of equal size.

"There were definitely sandwiches and loaves before the po'boy was invented, but that consistent 36-inch loaf was not invented until 1929 by John Gendusa," Parkway Bakery & Tavern general manager Justin Kennedy says. "I'm pretty confident of that."

The Martin brothers' and John Gendusa's contributions in 1929 popularized a sandwich that has truly become "the people's food." Just like red beans and gumbo, po'boys are what keep New Orleanians of any social class and background going. It has become a true equalizer within the Big Easy.

"Really, it's something we all come together over," Whann says. "Doesn't matter what neighborhood, what ward you come from. It doesn't matter where you went to school. Everyone loves po'boys. And I think we're all looking for common ground. We're all looking for something that brings us together. I think the po'boy does that. I think it's a cultural treasure. I think the support for the po'boy festival on Oak Street is an example of that."

"The thing about a po'boy shop, especially here in New Orleans, I would say like these old shops, every walk of life comes here . . . I say, '8 to 80, cripple to crazy,'" Kennedy explains. "And I've said this a hundred times, you'll see a man with a $500 suit at the bar sitting next to a guy who's like in construction or just in a ratty old shirt, and they're eating the same sandwich: shrimp po'boy. And they make friends. They start talking about what's going on. You hardly see that anywhere else. I think it's just the cuisine and, what it is, it's a sandwich that everybody enjoys."

There are even instances where the Martin brothers' original action of helping "poor boys" who are in need with a sandwich is still going on almost one hundred years after the fact.

"We get a few drifters who come by, and they're homeless and they ask for food, and I'll give them a cold-cut po'boy . . . that's what they need," the president and owner of Short Stop Poboys, Russell Hendrick, says. "They need nourishment, so I'll just give them a sandwich, which is probably what happened back then."

Because of the Martin brothers working to help serve their community, the po'boy has become not just a sandwich. It is now a cultural icon of New Orleans, one with history and a direct tie to the people who call the Crescent City home.

"It's culture you can eat," Kennedy says. "It's like an edible museum. I mean, there's history around it. There's a reason why it's here."

French bread loaves from John Gendusa Bakery.

# 3

# New Orleans French Bread and the Historic Bakeries That Make It

France governed the Louisiana colony for less than one hundred years, yet the country's legacy is firmly entrenched in both southern Louisiana and New Orleans. Louisiana French is still being kept alive in certain regions of the state, French Acadian and French Creole music (Cajun and zydeco, respectively) are celebrated genres within the state, the territorial divisions of the state are still called parishes rather than counties, and the fleur-de-lis symbol is practically all over Greater New Orleans and Acadiana. So it should come as no surprise that this area of the United States has its own version of one of the most quintessential French creations: the baguette.

The baguette, along with escargot and frog legs, is generally what people might picture in their minds when they think about French cuisine. Simply put, the French love baguettes, which are made from lean dough and are best known for their crispy crust and large length. According to Jim Chevallier's *About the Baguette: Exploring the Origin of a French National Icon,* these types of bread seem to have been present in France since at least the seventeenth century, meaning that baguette-like long bread was in the country when it established French Louisiana in 1682.

However, when looking at a baguette and Louisiana French bread, while they are both noticeably similar, there are still some differences. Two of the best people in New Orleans who are able to tell the difference between the two breads are the owners of two of the oldest bakeries in the Crescent City: Leidenheimer Baking Company and John Gendusa Bakery.

Sandy Whann, who has been president of Leidenheimer Baking Company since the early 1990s, clarifies how New Orleans French bread is different from a baguette because of its light interior crumb and thin, crisp crust. "The difference with New Orleans French bread vs. a Parisian baguette is that our bread tends to be much lighter," Whann explains. "The crust is not as thick and the crumb is not as dense as what you would typically find in Europe, although I have had baguettes in France that come pretty close to ours in terms of lightness, but, typically, they tend to be heavier and more dense."

Jason Gendusa, baker and owner of John Gendusa Bakery for over twenty years, says the French bread's light interior actually helps with the po'boy's taste since it does not overpower the flavors of the sandwich's fillings. "When you slice it open, it's nice and airy and thin inside," Gendusa says. "That way when you put whatever you're putting on the sandwich, you can actually taste what you're eating instead of just bread. It holds up well, even though it's light."

Gendusa says if a heavier bread, like for example a sourdough, is used instead of French bread, the results would not be the same.

"You can throw whatever on there, but all you do taste is bread the whole time you're eating it," Gendusa says.

It's very important to remember that, if the po'boy bread does not have an identifiably crispy exterior and fluffy interior, then it's not considered a "traditional-style" New Orleans French bread.

"If it's real doughy, if it's heavy bread, it's wrong," Joanne Domilise, general manager of Domilise's Po-Boy & Bar, says. "Definitely wrong. That bread is key. That's what makes a po'boy."

"I think French bread is the medium," Russell Hendrick, president and owner of Short Stop Poboys, says. "If it wasn't for that, where would we be? I just don't see serving sourdough po'boys. We have a luxury here having French bread the way we have it."

"The bread is more important than the filling," Eric Baucom, chef, owner, and operator of Killer PoBoys, says. "The bread's the frame to the whole thing. Without the bread, it's not a po'boy."

Another major difference between French bread and the baguette is that the two breads are made for different climates. Southern Louisiana's heat and humidity makes it so that French bread actually absorbs moisture in the air during the hotter months of the year.

"When it is very hot and humid, we actually have to bake the product longer in order to dry out the bread a little more because the bread is going to act as a sponge and the humidity is going to be absorbed by the bread throughout the day, particularly during the delivery process, and so that bread will tend to get softer and softer," Whann says. "Conversely in the winter, we tend to bake the bread less because the lack of humidity is going to harden the crust throughout the day. So yes, we absolutely have to adapt and adjust not only with the bake but it can also be with the amount of water or yeast that we put into the bread as well, just to make sure that we're taking into account all those various conditions."

An important element of French bread to be aware of is that, if it is bought and left out to sit in, say, a kitchen for an entire day, the loaf will be completely hardened the next day, thus losing its fluffy interior.

"The whole point of French bread is that it is a one-day product 'cause with that harder outer shell, the longer the day goes by, the harder it gets," Gendusa explains.

While it does not have a really long shelf life, French bread can actually be put in a freezer and rewarmed at a later date, if desired. If handled correctly, the reheated loaf can be about as good as when it was first bought.

"It freezes well," Gendusa says. "It's a good product to freeze, take out, stick in the oven, and you'll think you've got a hot bread from the bakery."

"We always recommend that you cut it to the desired length and, if possible, wrap it in plastic and put it into a freezer bag," Whann says. "If that's done, it will last for an incredibly long time. Up to three or four months. And then when you take it out, you actually keep it frozen and you put it in the oven. Directly on the rack, not in a pan, at 350 degrees. That fact that it goes in there frozen will help retain moisture during the process of heating. People have great success with this. You'll get that crisp crust and that light, airy interior when you do that, even after it's been frozen for a few months."

Leidenheimer Baking Company can attest to how well French bread can be reheated even after being frozen because the bakery actually has national distribution, where its French bread is shipped to various distributors across the United States.

"Our bread ships frozen through food service distributors, really, across the country," Whann says. "We have many, many frozen distributors such as Sysco and US Foods and other distributors who buy our product and then deliver to customers directly. And the product—it obviously requires some additional handling and care. But when it's done correctly, it's really a wonderful result. It's really a thrill to have the product served in states all over. We're in about thirty states right now."

Speaking of states, French bread is not exclusive to just New Orleans. There are numerous bakeries across Louisiana that specialize in baking their own loaves, like Hi-Do Bakery in Terrytown and LeJeune's Bakery Inc. in Jeanerette. However, just because French bread can be found throughout the state does not necessarily mean that all of the loaves are exactly the same.

Whann says New Orleans French bread is just one of the many types of French bread that can be found within Louisiana and that the bread is baked differently depending on what region the product is in.

"That French bread is only made in New Orleans because that's what New Orleans restaurants and sandwich shops and po'boy lovers want," Whann explains. "The French bread that is made in Lafayette is not New Orleans French bread. Never has been, never will be. It is a softer crust. It is a different bread. It's not the bread New Orleanians are accustomed to, nor is our French bread what people in Lafayette or North Louisiana are accustomed to. So it's a regional formula. It's a regional product. So can New Orleans French bread be made outside of New Orleans? I'm sure it can. The bigger issue is: each region has its own specific characteristics of that French bread, and a baker who wants to be successful and remain in business is going to make a product that that market demands."

Sometimes, using the same equipment and techniques to make French bread in a different location can result in a completely altered product.

"Just from an experience in our bakery when my father first took over, he was hired by a place in Houston to make bread for them there," Gendusa says. "It was a long, drawn-out process. They got all the same equipment that he had at the bakery here in New Orleans and they set it up exactly like it was. Mirror image. He went over there—I think he even brought one of his best bakers. And they could not replicate it to save themselves. They say the water, humidity, all that has a lot to do with it."

Both Leidenheimer Baking Company and John Gendusa Bakery have been key players in keeping French bread alive and thriving within and outside of New Orleans for a very long time. Ironically, the two classic bakeries, located in America's most French city and known best for their French bread, were not founded by Frenchmen. Leidenheimer was originated by a German baker named George Leidenheimer, and Gendusa Bakery was established by a Sicilian baker named John Gendusa, both arriving as immigrants to a city that was culturally diverse even in the late nineteenth and early twentieth centuries.

According to Whann, some of the reasons George Leidenheimer came to settle in New Orleans was to escape from a difficult period in Germany's history, as well as to be with family who were already in the city.

"If my history is correct, that was a time of great upheaval in Germany, and I think that, at least according to family lore, he left because he didn't want to be conscripted into the army," Whann says. "The Franco-Prussian War had happened during what probably would have been his early childhood and I think that's the main reason that he came to the States, and he came to New Orleans because of the vibrancy and the size of the German community, as well as the fact that he had family here."

According to "German Culture in New Orleans" on NewOrleans. com, tens of thousands of German immigrants had been moving to New Orleans since the mid-1800s. When Leidenheimer arrived in the city, he at first worked as a baker for some of his relatives who already had a bakery set up.

"He came to the United States from Deidesheim, Germany, in the 1880s," Whann says. "His family had been involved in the baking business in Germany, and he actually had relatives who were in the baking business here and he worked for them for a bit. Then he started his own bakery in 1896 and it was located on Dryades Street. In fact, it was located near the Southern Food and Beverage Museum and his stables were actually right next to the museum."

Before automobiles became a widespread method of transportation in the early twentieth century, animal-drawn carriages and wagons were used to transport not only people, but products as well. "The wagons he used to deliver the bread were all drawn by horses or mules, and bakers had to have stalls to keep their livestock in," Whann explains. "We still have stables here at our bakery, as having the animals to help with the delivery was a key part of the bakery business."

According to Whann, George Leidenheimer built part of the building Leidenheimer Baking Company is currently in, located at 1501 Simon Bolivar Avenue. The company moved into that building in 1905, and it's been there ever since. In the beginning, Leidenheimer produced heavy breads that he and the local German community were used to eating in their homeland.

"If you could imagine the early 1900s, you still had a variety of ethnic neighborhoods that were primarily populated by Germans, Irish, Italians, etc.," Whann says. "Many of the bakers, whether they were German or Italian or others, were making breads from their homelands. So Leidenheimer, obviously in those early days, was involved in baking many of the heavy, dense breads of his native Germany. But over time, particularly given the French influence and the Spanish influence in the city, the bread offering began to change and the bread got lighter and lighter in order to appeal to the palates of the residents in New Orleans."

According to Leidenheimer Baking Company's website, the bakery has a long and varied list of breads that it distributes to a number of different local restaurants and grocery stores, as well as nationally. Including French bread, Leidenheimer also offers goods like gourmet hamburger buns, bread crumbs, and muffuletta loaves. A muffuletta is another famed New Orleans sandwich that has origins in the city's Sicilian community and uses sliced Italian meats, cheeses, and a topping New Orleanians call "olive salad," which is diced olives and pickled vegetables that are marinated in olive oil. That sandwich is put together using a large, round sesame bread that is horizontally split.

An important part of Leidenheimer Baking Company, which actually turned 125 years old in 2021, is that the bakery has been family owned and operated since the very beginning, with Sandy Whann being the fourth generation of his family to run the company. According to Whann, George Leidenheimer had one daughter, named Josephine, who was very young when her father passed away. Her cousins then ran the bakery until she married Robert J. Whann Jr., who then ran the business until the early 1970s. Upon his death, Sandy Whann's father, Robert J. Whann III, took it over from him. Sandy joined his dad in the business in 1986 and has been there ever since.

"He and I worked together until about 2004 when he retired and I've run the business with my sister, Katherine, and my brother-in-law, Mitch Abide," Whann says. "He oversees all of our operations. My sister handles the administrative side."

According to Whann, his son, William Whann, joined the bakery in 2020 and will be the fifth generation of his family to run the company. Whann says the theme of family is not only important to Leidenheimer Baking Company, but also to the city of New Orleans as well.

"I think it means everything," Whann says. "It's not just the Whann family, but it's the many, many families who've worked here over the years. Obviously, the workforce has changed quite a bit with COVID. But throughout my career, we've been blessed to have many families who've had multiple family members working for the company for generations. Of course, our family has a great deal of pride in this business. New Orleans is filled with family businesses. Many of them are in the food business, restaurant business, etc. I've always been involved with a family business, so I really don't know anything else. But I do know that when your name is on the door, you do take a great deal of pride in what you do and you take a great deal of care and concern for your own customers and you try to treat them like family as well. I can't say enough about it. I know that family is the reason that I'm in this industry."

A consistent theme throughout New Orleans's history is resilience. Not only has the city seen a number of wars, but its location near large bodies of water has made it a breeding ground for diseases like yellow fever, which had an outbreak in the city in 1853. There were two great fires in 1788 and in 1794 that almost completely destroyed the French Quarter. The Crescent City is also often in the direct pathway of hurricanes, which can cause enormous damage. Of course the worst was Hurricane Katrina in 2005, one of the deadliest and most costly storms ever to hit the United States. That storm caused the deaths of hundreds upon hundreds of New Orleanians and forced many residents to leave their city and never return. The ones who endured the ordeal and stayed in New Orleans all have a story of survival in their histories.

According to Whann, he and Ralph Brennan, who is the head of the Ralph Brennan Restaurant Group, were both with their families in Baton Rouge when Katrina hit.

"Ralph and I got back into town probably ten days after the storm, I guess," Whann says. "We were able to get to our houses and businesses and we had some damage that we were able to get a contractor to start fixing, but, of course, we didn't have power . . . coming into the plant itself on that first day back, the smell was pretty eye-opening. We didn't have much of an emergency plan back then. I don't think many people did. When I got back into the bakery in early September, we had about 5,000 pounds of yeast, compressed, refrigerated yeast, that had melted. The smell of 5,000 pounds of melted yeast that had been sitting in the heat for weeks covering your floors is not something you want to walk into. So you can imagine the clean-up we had. It was a lengthy process, but everybody pitched in."

A major challenge that Whann faced while restarting Leidenheimer Baking Company was that his employees were spread all over Louisiana due to evacuating and they did not have anywhere to stay in New Orleans due to many of their homes being damaged.

"We actually had housing here on-site for some of our employees; we had trailers," Whann says. "We actually ran a van to Baton Rouge to some of the various shelters to pick up our employees and brought them into work and then brought them back."

Luckily, Leidenheimer Baking Company was able to completely rebuild, showing how resilient the Crescent City and its citizens have consistently been for over three hundred years.

"We were able to reopen in October," Whann says. "Within about two years, we were back to our pre-Katrina sales levels, but it was quite an event. It took a few years off of my life, I'm sure. But it really highlighted the incredible flexibility and dedication of our workforce and that of our customers . . . we're a resilient place. We've been kicked to the ground before; we always seem to get up. I think that says a lot about our citizens and it says a lot about our businesses. You know, a lot of these businesses are family and family businesses have a lot of motivation for getting back up and going as quickly as possible."

Like Leidenheimer, John Gendusa Bakery also has a long history in New Orleans, is still family owned and operated, and was started by an immigrant to the city. According to Jason Gendusa, his great-grandfather, John Gendusa, moved from Sicily to New Orleans in the early 1920s and started out baking bread in a local grocery store. His skills with bread developed in his homeland proved to be very beneficial for him.

"People loved it. That kinda overtook the grocery store," Gendusa says.

John Gendusa ended up purchasing the grocery he worked for and officially opened John Gendusa Bakery at 2009 Mirabeau Avenue in New Orleans's Gentilly neighborhood in 1922. The bakery's biggest claim to fame is being the originator of the uniform French bread loaf that John Gendusa developed for the Martin brothers during the 1929 streetcar strike, thus setting the standard for what po'boy bread would be from then on. In addition, the bakery successfully reached its one-hundredth anniversary in 2022.

"I think it's one of those things I might look back on and be like, 'Wow. That's pretty amazing,'" Gendusa says. "I think any business that can sustain for one hundred years, obviously you must be doing something right, especially in a food town like New Orleans. I guess our French bread withstood the test of time. So yeah, it's definitely pretty cool."

In addition to baking French bread, which, according to Gendusa, is sold wholesale and distributed throughout many restaurants in New Orleans, Baton Rouge, and the Mississippi Gulf Coast, John Gendusa Bakery also makes dinner rolls, hamburger buns, and classic NOLA-Sicilian muffuletta bread.

"We've been doing that for as long as I can remember and probably as long as a muffuletta has been around . . . ninety-five percent of what we sell is the muffuletta and the French bread," Gendusa says.

According to Gendusa, the recipes for the bakery's different breads have not really changed since his great-grandfather started the business.

"My dad used to always tell me that when things go bad, if you change it up, go back to how we used to do it one hundred years ago, and it's a proven formula," Gendusa says.

Gendusa says while the process of actually baking French bread is not that difficult in and of itself, the most challenging aspect of the loaves is making sure that every single detail involved with the process is correct so that the bread comes out perfect.

"The process itself isn't strenuous, but it's very detail oriented," Gendusa explains. "From the mixing that has to be done just right to the way the dough runs through the machine and then when the guys get it and do the handwork on it, it all has to be done very detailed or else you won't get a good loaf of bread."

According to Gendusa, his bakery has always operated on a somewhat smaller scale, but he is hoping to be able to expand and bring in some more automated elements to help with production in the future, especially since the bakery gets plenty of requests for more national distribution. However, Gendusa stresses that he does not want to eliminate the human element that he says is needed to make a great loaf of New Orleans French bread.

"I do find when you have the right people, it's always better than a machine," Gendusa says. "A person can put a little TLC into what they're doing. So you don't want to eliminate that aspect, but we would like to get to the point where we can get a little bit of both. A little more automated, a little more efficient, but still keep that hands-on approach, to keep the product coming out as it's been for the last one hundred years."

That one hundred years in business was certainly tested when the levees surrounding the London Avenue Canal were breached during Hurricane Katrina, dumping an astronomical amount of flood-water into the Gentilly neighborhood where John Gendusa Bakery is located.

"We're about six blocks from where the levee broke right down on Mirabeau," Gendusa says. "I mean, we had nine feet of water. There was nothing salvageable in here and we had a lot of sleepless nights thinking about what to do."

Gendusa says what really helped to kick off rebuilding the bakery was actually members of the community giving the Gendusa family their support.

"We were in here cleaning up and it was an older gentleman who stopped in," Gendusa details. "And he said, 'I know y'all aren't making any bread. You have any idea when?' My father was here and he said, 'You know, we really don't know what we're going to do.' He was like, 'Man, me and my family grew up on your product. You can't go anywhere. You really need to do it for the city.' When I heard him say that, it kinda like flipped that switch in my head. I was like, 'You know, what? It's time to get rolling.'"

Some community members even offered to take more active roles in helping the Gendusa family.

"Anything we needed, people would come by," Gendusa says. "'Do you need us to come in here with a forklift and move stuff for you?' I mean, people were just very helpful and that helped also with the decision to rebuild."

According to Gendusa, his family even received assistance from outside of Louisiana.

"We had a really good guy up in New Jersey who shipped us an oven and a mixer and he said, 'Pay us when you can,'" Gendusa says. "That got us started with that."

The bakery was out of commission for a year after Katrina hit, according to Gendusa, mainly because the family did not have anywhere to live in New Orleans due to extensive damage. Despite not being centrally located near the bakery at that time (Gendusa was in Baton Rouge, and his parents were in Florida), the bakery was able to be rebuilt and survive because of the Gendusa family's dedication to serving the city they call home.

"What keeps us going is we got a deep root in the city's history and people enjoy it," Gendusa says. "Those are the reasons why we keep on moving along."

In addition to providing a quality product to his customers in

Louisiana and Mississippi, Gendusa says another aspect he is thankful for is that the bakery has been a family owned and operated business for so long.

"My whole life, I've worked with my mother and father side-by-side," Gendusa says. "They're definitely getting up there in age, but they still come every day and help out a couple hours a day. It's always helpful to have that extra set of hands; in the case of my father, the knowledge. If I run into problems or issues, it's always helpful to be able to talk to him about it . . . especially in a family business, it's helpful to always have those extra people around."

Gendusa says while he would like to have his children continue the family legacy of running John Gendusa Bakery, he would also like to make the entire process a bit easier for them to just walk in and run it smoothly if they choose to do it. According to the bakery's website, not only does Gendusa serve as the owner and as a baker, he also handles the bakery's office work, equipment and truck repairs, and much more. Gendusa says he puts in a minimum of thirteen or fourteen hours a day while on the job.

No matter what the future has in store for John Gendusa Bakery, Gendusa says knowing people love the French bread that his bakery produces, the same French bread that assisted in turning the humble po'boy into a historic staple of New Orleans cuisine, helps him and his team keep the business going and encourages them to put a lot of heart and soul into what they do.

"The best thing that I get out of this is when people tell me how good the bread is," Gendusa says. "It just makes you feel good 'cause you know New Orleanians, they're big on their food. So when they tell you something is good, that goes a long way and that helps me get up every morning to do this."

Both John Gendusa Bakery and Leidenheimer Baking Company have done a tremendous job withstanding the test of time and staying in operation for over one hundred years. Unfortunately, many of the other French bread bakeries that had a noticeable presence in New Orleans did not make it long enough to experience the same milestone.

"Just going back twenty years, I could think there were seven of us," Gendusa says. "Now there's two of us. That's a big loss in just twenty years to lose half of the bakeries in the city."

One bakery that New Orleanians of a certain age are all too familiar with was Reising's Bakery, which had its brand of French bread and other products housed in supermarkets all over New Orleans. Whann says he and his family had personal history with Reising's Bakery while it was still around in the city.

"We were family friends for many, many years with the owners of Reising's," Whann says. "It was owned by the Salmon family. In fact, they owned the original Sunbeam Bakery here in New Orleans and I grew up working for them in the summer. When they sold Sunbeam, they ended up buying Reising's Bakery from the founder, Andy Reising, and they ran that company in the mid-'80s through the early '90s."

According to Whann, Reising's Bakery, which primarily specialized in French bread and pistolets, had a significant presence in New Orleans's supermarket industry during its existence. From the time the Salmon family acquired Reising's, the supermarket industry went through a lot of changes, which led to Reising's ultimately

Reising's French bread from Leidenheimer Baking Company.

being bought and consolidated into Leidenheimer in January 1990. Despite Reising's no longer being around, Whann says Leidenheimer Baking Company has put in the effort to keep Reising's products alive to this day.

"We acquired them in 1990 and what we did was we took over their brands in the grocery stores," Whann explains. "We continued to deliver Reising's brand of product into stores because their customer base is so loyal to them. Just as Leidenheimer's is to us. So we decided to maintain both brands and we still do to this day. Basically, we brought over a number of their employees, a number of their salesmen, and, obviously, it was a major boost to Leidenheimer's business. I really credit that acquisition with putting us on the healthy path that we're fortunate to be on today."

Another local French bread bakery, Angelo Gendusa Bakery, was also consolidated into Leidenheimer Baking Company in 2004, and that establishment, according to Gendusa, actually broke off from his family's bakery in the first half of the twentieth century.

"They branched out from my great-grandfather way back in the maybe '30s or '40s," Gendusa says. "So that was one time our family bakery as well."

One of the most recent bakeries that disappeared from the city was Alois J. Binder Bakery, which was located on 940 Frenchmen Street. Owned and operated by the Binder family since 1914, the bakery, according to its website, delivered its French bread to various restaurants, groceries, and hotels in Greater New Orleans. Despite Leidenheimer trying for many years to acquire Binder's like Reising's and Angelo Gendusa's, according to Whann, the bakery's owners just refused to sell it. In September 2018, Alois J. Binder Bakery ended up closing its doors, leaving only Leidenheimer Baking Company and John Gendusa Bakery as the last traditional French bread bakers in New Orleans.

"That company simply did not open one morning and just disappeared, which was very sad because their products were extremely high quality," Whann says.

Whann says it is hard to think about how Binder's, as well as all of the other multigenerational businesses, just went away after being such a major presence in the city for many years.

"It makes me sad," Whann says. "I loved having Binder's there.

They were a great competitor. Honest, ethical, and high-quality producer. I personally hated to see them go. I tried to prevent it, but it didn't work out."

With New Orleans down to only two local, family-owned French bread bakeries as of 2022, it's not too far-fetched to imagine the loaves have become kind of "threatened," at least in terms of the bread's production within the city. Whann says one reason he feels traditional New Orleans French bread has received a somewhat endangered status within New Orleans proper is because he believes the city has not seen a major population growth in a number of decades, thus limiting the size of the bakery industry.

"The population has not grown in New Orleans for decades," Whann says. "It's not surprising at all that the independent bakers have either gone away or things have been consolidated. I don't think it has anything to do with the lack of people's desire for traditional New Orleans French bread. I think it's very, very strong. You just have fewer people and, at the very least, a stagnant population that's not growing. And our business thrives on mouths to feed, whether it's in restaurants or groceries or in po'boy shops."

So when New Orleanians are adamant about "supporting local," it comes from a place where they know that their longstanding businesses could just vanish in a blink of an eye and another piece of the city's unique culture could be lost forever. If there is no French bread, there are no po'boys. That is the harsh reality of things, and it is what makes the idea of New Orleans losing any more of its bakeries an incredibly scary possibility.

Whann thinks that, with the loss of most of the local family-operated bakeries within the city, it is absolutely critical that po'boys and New Orleans French bread receive some kind of preservation treatment, especially since national sandwich chains have the financial and marketing strength to easily get customers into their shops.

"You've had a huge growth in the national sandwich-shop chain business, but they don't reflect the culture and traditions of New Orleans the way that our independent po'boy shops do," Whann says. "I think, just like our music, our cuisine is critical to our identity, and I can't imagine anything that would sadden me more than for future generations to not understand how the New Orleans po'boy has been something that's been special in this city generation after generation. It's brought people together as much as any other cuisine that the city is known for. I absolutely believe that the hard-working folks who run our independent po'boy shops and neighborhood restaurants in the city of New Orleans are carrying that flag and they're keeping it alive for future generations, maintaining incredibly high quality, using local purveyors, bread, seafood, condiments, and produce. And I think that speaks volumes."

One way Whann himself has tried to help keep po'boys and French bread visible in the city was when he helped to establish the New Orleans Po'Boy Preservation Society in the early 2000s with his sister, Katherine, and some of NOLA's best-known po'boy shop owners. Whann says he started the society to sound the alarm to local family-owned and independently owned po'boy shops regarding just how important they were to the Crescent City.

"The core reason for my founding this was to have the po'boy shops try to band together and say, 'Hey, we are New Orleans culture, and we need to let everybody know in the city who loves po'boys and loves New Orleans culture and cuisine that we need your support,'" Whann says.

Another way Whann says the society has helped with keeping French bread and po'boys alive within New Orleans was when it first planted the seeds of having a festival solely dedicated to the sandwich. The idea would first take shape in 2007 as the New Orleans Po'Boy Preservation Festival, which has since morphed into the Oak Street Po'Boy Festival.

"When we first had the idea for the Po'Boy Fest, it was in a year or so prior to Katrina," Whann says. "I was in a meeting with the owners of Parkway Bakery, and we talked about having a festival that celebrated the po'boy and let New Orleans know what a local treasure we had and that it needed support in order to survive."

The festival initially had a major focus on the history and preservation of NOLA's favorite sandwich and its bread through panel discussions with some of the city's leading authorities on the subject, according to Gendusa.

"I was there, my father, Sandy Whann from Leidenheimer, Tom Fitzmorris," Gendusa says. "It was actually like a discussion panel, and people came in and we talked about it and the ways that we could preserve it."

The festival, which is currently organized by the nonprofit Oak Street Merchants, Residents, and Property Owners organization as of 2022, now has a greater focus of stimulating and promoting the historic Oak Street Corridor located between South Carrollton Avenue and Leake Street in Uptown New Orleans, according to the festival's website. However, the main draw to the festival is still the po'boy, with crowds into the thousands flocking to the festival each year to celebrate and enjoy a sandwich that is deeply ingrained in the Crescent City's history and culture.

"It shows that the passion is very much there for the po'boy and, as importantly, for the people who make them because they're wonderful characters as well," Whann says. "That's really what New Orleans is about. It's great food and the great personalities who make it."

The biggest factors in helping preserve both French bread and po'boys in New Orleans really are the people who work long and hard to create these items every single day. While John Gendusa Bakery and Leidenheimer Baking Company are the last of the historical bakeries left in NOLA and they maintain a healthy competition with each other, they also take the time to support each other if one of them is in any sort of need, according to Gendusa.

"We help each other out anyway we can if one of us is short on something or needs anything, you know?" Gendusa says. "There's never been any issue with either one of us helping each other out. There's not too many of us, so we kinda need to stick together."

With how important French bread is to New Orleanians, those crispy and airy loaves, and the bakeries that still make them, will hopefully continue to persevere and satisfy the city for another one hundred and more years.

Roast beef po'boy from Short Stop Poboys.

# 4

# Experiencing All Sides of the Po'Boy

## *Spots to Get a Good Sandwich or Two*

It might be a bit of hyperbole, but if someone were financially stable enough to eat at a different New Orleans–based restaurant every night, it might take him or her close to a year to try them all. Of all of New Orleans's well-known attributes, its eateries are perhaps the city's most distinguished accomplishments. From the historic Creole restaurants like Arnaud's and Antoine's (which is one of the oldest operating restaurants in the United States, having been established in 1840) to the many different shops selling more humble creations like muffulettas and sno-balls (shaved ice with syrup), it's difficult to know exactly where to start.

Limiting oneself to just po'boys does not make the decisions any easier. There are too many restaurants around the Big Easy that have at least some po'boys on their menus, and they are all good in their own way. However, there are a few places both inside and outside of New Orleans that showcase different aspects of what a po'boy is all about: its history, how the sandwich can build connections between people, how it's popular enough to spread outside of New Orleans, how it still serves a purpose of helping its local community, and how much creativity can be shown by treating French bread like a painter's canvas. Some of these shops are around one hundred years old, and others have a more recent history, but they are all good at what they do, which is providing quality po'boys to locals and tourists alike.

One of the best places to savor the historical aspect of po'boys is one of the oldest po'boy shops in all of New Orleans. Located at 538 Hagan Avenue in the Bayou St. John neighborhood of Mid-City New Orleans is **Parkway Bakery & Tavern**, one of the most recognizable po'boy shops in the entire city. Justin Kennedy, general manager of Parkway Bakery, says the restaurant was founded over one hundred years ago, and the layout of the building reflects its age.

"If you look at Parkway, it has that unique New Orleans corner-cut, tin awning, a door on the corner," Kennedy explains. "You got those kinds of buildings speckled all over the city. Back in the old days, those buildings were corner bakeries, corner groceries, corner delis because you didn't have supermarkets, and Parkway was a bakery. It opened up in 1911 from a German baker named Charles Goering."

According to Parkway's website, Goering Sr. ran the business until it was purchased in 1922 by Henry Timothy Sr., who continued using Parkway as a bakery through the 1920s to produce bread, doughnuts, and sweet rolls. Kennedy says Parkway did not start doing po'boys until after John Gendusa developed the uniform French bread loaf for the Martin brothers during the 1929 streetcar strike.

"All of these other bakeries in town, when they saw how popular it was, started doing the same thing and Parkway was one of them," Kennedy says. "So we kinda like jumped on the bandwagon and then we started serving the sandwiches."

According to Kennedy, the Timothy family, which included Henry Sr. and his sons Henry Jr. and Jake, who both took over the business in the 1960s, really made a name for Parkway from the 1920s to the 1970s when they got into the po'boy business. During that time, the neighborhood that surrounded Parkway was very industrial. Not only were there a number of warehouses, there was also the Southern Railroad Line (which is currently a linear public park called the Lafitte Greenway) and the American Can Company (which is currently the American Can Apartment complex on Orleans Avenue). Workers from all of these different businesses served as Parkway's primary customer base.

"They'd blow the whistle in the American Can Company, those guys would line up, and you better knew what you wanted because [the Timothys] were, I wouldn't say rough, but they were tough guys," Kennedy says. "That's how you had to be back then. If you stuttered, they'd kick you out of line. Next."

Parkway's website even shows glimpses of the restaurant's past during the time of the Timothy family, including a picture of two men eating po'boys and sitting in front of one of the restaurant's windows, which has the message "Poor Boy Sandwiches: 10 cents" on it, while also advertising a "combination."

"You don't hear it as much, but a 'combination' is a fried ham and cheese," Kennedy says. "Flat, griddled, sliced ham and melted cheese on it."

Despite many years of prosperity under the Timothy family, Parkway eventually ended up falling on hard times.

"Fast forward to like the '80s and the '90s, things started to slow down," Kennedy explains. "The can company had closed down. The Southern Railroad had shut down. All this industry had dried up."

Without the business they once had, Jake and Henry Timothy Jr. first tried to operate with reduced hours, according to Parkway's website, until 1993, when they decided to shut the business down and put it up for sale. The next chapter of Parkway's history began when a man named Jay Nix, who is Kennedy's uncle, moved from Uptown to Mid-City in the 1990s.

"The old guys ended up selling the place to my uncle, Jay Nix, who was a contractor," Kennedy says. "He lived right next door to the restaurant . . . when it went up for sale, he didn't buy it to reopen it. He needed more space for all of his equipment and his construction stuff."

According to Kennedy, his uncle would often bring him to the restaurant, which was in a major state of disrepair, so that he could help him get tools for different construction jobs.

"I would work with my uncle and his construction business when I was eight, nine, ten years old," Kennedy says. "We'd go into the restaurant and get saws and tools to go to the job site. Wherever we worked in the metro area, if he saw an old-timer with some age on him, he'd bring up that his toolshed was the old Parkway, and they would tell him stories, 'Man, they had the best hot sausage, the best oyster sandwiches, the best roast beef.' So I guess like ten years after hearing all of that, he said, 'Man, I need to open this place back up.'"

With the decision made, Nix put in the money to restore Parkway Bakery & Tavern to working order, and the restaurant officially reopened on December 22, 2003.

"We didn't know what we were doing," Kennedy explains. "I was a kid and Jay was used to construction. He had never been in the restaurant business. We had hired managers and hired people to help us get it going and they did. The first day we opened, line out the door. I remember that. Line out the door. From just like people who wanted to relive their childhood and then like grandparents who wanted to take their kids to the old Parkway. You know, they never got a chance to witness something like this."

According to Parkway's website, Nix and Kennedy made the decision to officially have all of their sandwiches be "poor boys" instead of po'boys to honor the striking streetcar workers from 1929 and recognize that the sandwich was born during a difficult period in history. In addition to a good selection of traditional style po'boys such as hot sausage patties and fried oysters, the shop also has more experimental po'boys like a vegetarian Italian Caprese, a three-foot-long Bayou Beast, and a po'boy named the James Brown, which is BBQ beef, fried shrimp, pepper jack cheese, and hot sauce mayo. According to Kennedy, Parkway actually won the 2018 edition of the Oak Street Po'Boy Festival with the James Brown poor boy. However, there are some Parkway po'boys that Kenney notices people tend to always gravitate towards.

"By far, shrimp and roast beef are the tops," Kennedy says. "Shrimp beats roast beef half of the year and roast beef beats shrimp half the year. Those two, we sell literally thousands a week."

Kennedy, who has also worked as Parkway's head chef, says what made him really fall in love with the po'boy shop was all the different people who came to Parkway and became regulars, especially the older customers who lived on his block right near the restaurant.

"They'd come to the bar and they'd hang out and I'd shoot the breeze with them," Kennedy says. "All of those people are dead and gone, and most of these houses now are rentals. Things just change, you know?"

One event that brought major change to not only Parkway, but also the entire city of New Orleans, was Hurricane Katrina. Just two years after the shop officially reopened, Katrina hit the city and forced Parkway to shutter its doors yet again. According to Kennedy, Nix had invested about half a million dollars into renovating the building before the storm came through, so there was debate on whether he would try to reopen it or not.

"He had full insurance, so he was thinking about cashing the insurance and paying off everything and just selling it because you didn't think the city was going to come back after that," Kennedy explains.

Kennedy, who was attending college at the University of New Orleans when Katrina came, ended up transferring to the University of Southern Mississippi for three months before making the decision to completely pull out of school and go back home on a little motorcycle with a tank of gas strapped to the backseat.

"I made it to New Orleans and I remember driving over the High Rise," Kennedy says. "That busy high rise with so many people and so many lights and action . . . nothing. No lights. You had a little glimmer downtown kind of by where the French Quarter was."

When Kennedy did arrive back in New Orleans, he was able to help convince Nix to restart Parkway.

"I told him, 'Man, I'm in it to do this with you,'" Kennedy says. "He didn't say no, so I pulled out of school and we started shoveling and cleaning. Just one step, one step, one step, and then we got to open. We opened back up December of 2005."

According to Kennedy, Parkway was actually somewhat easy to get started again because of the renovations that were done to the building for the restaurant's first reopening in 2003.

"We were pretty much brand-new construction, the place was totally redone," Kennedy explains. "A lot of these places that got water, you know, they hadn't opened the walls or changed the electric or did anything in one hundred years, right? So they found all kinds of issues they had to redo. But us? We were pretty much brand new, so it was really easy to get the place cleaned up and back going again."

After reopening again in 2005, Parkway Bakery & Tavern has not slowed down since and just continues to grow in popularity. According to Parkway's website, the restaurant serves an average of one thousand customers per day.

"There was a warehouse that wrapped the building and it ended up being torn down by FEMA, and we ended up buying it," Kennedy says. "So that's our big parking lot that we have now and, since COVID, we have a drive-thru, like a preorder drive-thru, and online ordering. It's just amazing."

While business has certainly been booming for Parkway since 2005, Kennedy says that there are no intentions to expand to multiple other locations. The restaurant's team is committed to that single location that has been standing and surviving in Mid-City for over one hundred years.

"People have tried to ask us to go to the Northshore, go to Covington, go to Metairie," Kennedy says. "And a lot of places end up doing that when they get popular . . . we've never done that . . . we've always stayed true to this corner and we always will. I feel like that's part of why it's so special. There's only one and it's done right."

According to Kennedy, a big plan for Parkway's future is to try and keep the business family owned and operated. Nix is still Parkway's sole owner as of 2022, but Kennedy says he will be ready to continue the po'boy shop's legacy when the time comes.

"We've got a good relationship: me, him, and my mother," Kennedy says. "I'm next to carry the torch when he's not carrying it anymore, so it will always be kept in the family."

Hopefully, Parkway Bakery & Tavern will be able to keep feeding its traditional and unique po'boys to the Mid-City community, as well as its many, many other customers from both in and out of New Orleans, for many more years to come.

\* \* \*

One of the most important aspects of food is bringing people together. Whether they be complete strangers sharing a space, friends looking to catch up, or family members coming together for lunch or supper, food has the power to unite people. Food is a necessity of life, but so are human connections, and that is especially truly in a city like New Orleans. The po'boy, in particular, is a perfect catalyst for forging relationships between all kinds of folks.

Located in the Uptown neighborhood at 5240 Annunciation Street, **Domilise's Po-Boy & Bar** has over one hundred years of bringing people together with po'boys and treating them like family. The restaurant was originally founded around 1918 by Peter Domilise as a neighborhood bar. According to Ken Domilise, who is the restaurant's co-owner and whose family is still in ownership of and running the establishment, his grandfather, who grew up in a corner grocery store across the street from the restaurant, was a Navy cook during World War I and opened Domilise's when he came back home from the war. According to Joanne Domilise, Ken's wife and Domilise's general manager, the restaurant did not start serving food to its community until a few years after it opened and, when it did, it did not start out with po'boys.

"When he came back and started it as a bar, they started cooking and selling to the people, and to the Riverfront, plate lunches," Joanne says.

"We assume it was just servicing the neighborhood, as well as the working community, which was the Riverfront," Ken says. "Longshoremen, stevedores, anyone affiliated with marine transportation. So it was started like that just to service this area."

Both Joanne and Ken say they're not completely sure when exactly Domilise's switched over from plate lunches to po'boys, but according to Joanne, it was friends of the Domilise family who actually started making the sandwiches in the shop. Despite not originally starting out with po'boys, Domilise's has not looked back since making the change. The po'boys that are currently served there have a traditional simplicity to them, such as the hot smoked sausage links po'boy, the turkey and ham po'boy, and the wiener po'boy.

"What we feel is our best product has been the traditional and the old-line basic 'blocking and tackling' types of po'boys," Ken explains. "Roast beef with gravy, fried shrimp, fried oysters, hamburgers."

"Our most popular po'boy is the fried shrimp, by far," Joanne says. "After that, it would be the roast beef and Swiss. We cook our own roast beef and gravy in-house. And after that, it's probably the 'half and half.' That's where you select two seafoods, which is usually fried shrimp and fried oysters."

Despite not knowing when Domilise's po'boys were first served, it is known that the ones on the restaurant's menu have been consistent for a long time. Inside the restaurant, there is a menu board that, according to Joanne, was written by nuns from the School Sisters of Notre Dame in the 1970s, and the contents on that board have stayed pretty much the same.

"They did that in either 1973 or 1974, and we use that same menu board today," Joanne says. "Of course, prices have changed, but basically, each of the offerings are the same. I think it's pretty awesome to have something from them."

This sense of keeping tradition alive is demonstrated by the fact that, for the over one hundred years that Domilise's has been in business, it has remained family owned and operated. In fact, like a lot of

Shrimp po'boy from Domilise's Po-Boy & Bar.

small mom-and-pop establishments in the early twentieth century, the family lived in a home directly connected to the restaurant, which was where both Ken and his father were born and raised. According to Ken, after his grandfather passed away in the late 1940s, Ken's father, Sam, took over the business after coming back from World War II. After that happened, an important figure also got involved with the restaurant and would forever change Domilise's into one of the best-known po'boy shops in all of New Orleans. This person was Ken's mother, Dorothy "Miss Dot" Domilise.

According to Ken, Miss Dot came into the establishment in 1965 and, by that time, Domilise's was far into the business of selling po'boys to the Uptown community. However, she was the one who really put Domilise's on the map, both before and after she took over ownership from her husband in 1981 when he passed away. According to Domilise's website, Miss Dot both lived in and worked at the restaurant for over seventy years.

"She just added her personality to it," Ken says. "She did a lot of work with the neighborhood, with everybody in the city. She was just a popular person."

According to both Ken and Joanne, one of Miss Dot's greatest attributes was just how much she loved her customers, no matter who they were. It did not matter if they were well-known names in New Orleans or just students from the local colleges close by Domilise's. Miss Dot treated everyone who came through the restaurant's doors like they were part of her family.

"She had people who would come in here, students from Tulane and Loyola, and lots of times, she wouldn't even charge them anything," Ken says. "She was just that type of person. She had a large following, and people came in, just repeatedly, just to see Miss Dot and talk to Miss Dot."

According to Ken and Joanne, the restaurant was like a continuous social event for Miss Dot, and it served as a way for her to connect with people in the NOLA community. There were even instances where she invited customers into the Domilise family's living room, which was connected to the restaurant and is now used for office space, and have them sit on the family's sofa just to chat and visit with her.

"It was a real social network for her," Ken says. "It was very important to her lifestyle. Her customer base was super important to her. They were like family."

"She would go to weddings, birthdays, their going-away parties, just everything," Joanne says. "Had Christmas gifts for them, and birthday gifts for the customers. They were definitely family to her."

Ken says some of his friends actually went to the restaurant one time to visit Miss Dot and found former New Orleans mayor Mitch Landrieu visiting with her in the family's home.

"Friends said that they came in one day to tell my mother hello, and they opened the door and the mayor and Senator Mary Landrieu, his sister, were just sitting in here and talking to her," Ken says. "She was friends with everybody and people enjoyed talking to her. They really did."

Joanne recalls one time when the Neville Brothers, one of New Orleans's most influential R&B and funk groups, actually came to Domilise's to bring Miss Dot to one of their recording sessions.

"They came in a limousine, picked her up, and brought her to the recording studio and recorded with her sitting there," Joanne details. "She was definitely very social. She loved this place, loved her customers, and really enjoyed all of that."

Other famous names that have walked through the restaurant's doors have included Emeril Lagasse, the Manning family, Ella Brennan, Dr. John, and even Bob Dylan and Anthony Bourdain. Joanne says whenever all of those known individuals came to Domilise's, they all were just normal folks looking to enjoy the shop's po'boys like everybody else.

"We found that all of those names, when they come in here, they're just some normal guy next door," Joanne says. "They really are."

Miss Dot's love and dedication to Domilise's was so immense that she never stopped pitching in her time toward the restaurant, even when she was close to the end of her life. Miss Dot, who is labeled a "Guardian of Tradition" on Domilise's website, passed away at ninety years old in 2013.

"She was doing this well into her eighties," Joanne says. "Cutting bread is a lot when you're eighty-eight, eighty-nine years old."

Even though Miss Dot was the most recognizable face associated with Domilise's, generations of her family have continued to keep the po'boy shop afloat. That has included extended family as well, such as Miss Dot's daughter-in-law, Patti "NuNu" Domilise, who started working at the restaurant in 1985 and would eventually take over managing it after Miss Dot. Joanne took over as Domilise's general manager right before NuNu passed away in 2014, making her and Ken the third generation of the family to run the restaurant. In fact, according to Joanne, the fifth generation of the Domilise family, Ken and Joanne's granddaughter and grandson, has already started to pitch in as well. The granddaughter even helped with taking orders in the restaurant during the COVID-19 pandemic and even was able to take orders on Domilise's computer.

"My granddaughter, who was seven at the time, helped us when we first came back from COVID and were doing take-out orders only," Joanne details. "I couldn't have done it without her. It was me, two other workers, and the seven-year-old. She's fabulous."

In addition to striving to keep the business within familial hands, the Domilise family has worked to keep the restaurant as traditional and familiar looking to their customers as much as possible. According to Ken, the building itself has not changed since it got rebuilt after Hurricane Betsy in 1965.

"Prior to Betsy, it was different, but it was damaged so heavily that they lowered the ceiling and they put paneling on the walls," Ken explains.

In fact, according to Joanne and Ken, some of the furniture pieces in Domilise's have never been replaced and have quite a bit of age to them.

"The bar is the original bar," Joanne explains. "We actually had a customer sit at the bar one day, and he said, 'You know, this bar is over one hundred years old.' And I said, 'That's what I understand.' I thought he meant the whole thing. He meant the physical bar. He said, 'No, I'm telling you. It is. I'm a furniture appraiser. I can look at the details and tell you this bar was built at the turn of the century.'"

"What I can remember as a kid was that people stood up at that bar," Ken details. "There were no stools, but there were cuspidors. Chewing tobacco was big back then . . . we had to clean those cuspidors every day because people were spitting in them."

Luckily for the furniture, as well as the po'boy shop's customers, Domilise's was actually spared a great deal of damage during Hurricane Katrina. According to Joanne, the restaurant was closed down for just under two months but received enough water damage that a lot of equipment needed to be replaced.

"It was not terrible here," Joanne says. "We saw much worse in our family by far. This was minor. Although the refrigerators and freezers were not fun for them to take care of after with all of that rotten food. They still talk about what they had to go through emptying that out."

The only other major physical change Domilise's went through in its history was a renovation job in 2015, but even then, the family made sure that everything in the restaurant remained exactly the same as it was for the sake of their customer base, some of whom have been coming to their po'boy shop for generations. According to Joanne and Ken, while the kitchen was completely updated with new equipment and stainless-steel walls, the rest of the interior was put back exactly how it was before the renovations in order to keep the original character and ambiance of the shop.

"We couldn't change anything," Ken says. "I mean those barstools are probably as old as I am. Those tables too. I mean I can remember them from when I was a kid."

"The instruction that the contractor was given was, 'When the customers walk in the door, we don't want them to know anything happened,' and yet they tore it down to the studs," Joanne explains. "That place was totally renovated; every single thing. The ceiling, the walls, everything except the floor . . . they put up paneling. Nobody puts up paneling today, but we had paneling. They got the same color paneling. It was perfect. So they did successfully accomplish their goal of making it look exactly the same."

This dedication to keeping Domilise's as original as it possibly can be, in terms of its look and the traditional nature of its po'boys, is of great importance to both Ken and Joanne.

"It's very important to us that it be original," Joanne says. "We feel like that's a responsibility to maintain."

"Joanne and I both think that we have a legacy to continue," Ken says. "You can feel like it's a slice of New Orleans history. You can come here and go back in time."

One of the main reasons that Domilise's has been able to continue its legacy for over one hundred years is because of its customer base. According to Ken and Joanne, they have seen older people who have been regulars at the restaurant for many, many years bring their kids and grandkids to the restaurant as a way of passing down the restaurant's po'boys to future generations. Joanne says seeing the excitement and gratitude Domilise's customers have even just being in line at the restaurant is enough to give her the energy to keep working and providing them the shop's traditional po'boys day after day.

"I always used to say that his mother absolutely loved the customer, but it wasn't until I did that job that I understood what that was all about," Joanne says. "It was because the customers here are wonderful."

Miss Dot forever left her mark on Domilise's Po-Boy & Bar with a legacy that is firmly intertwined with family, both with her actual family continuing to keep the business open, as well as the customers she treated as such. The easiest way for families to come together is over food, and Domilise's po'boys have been creating connections within New Orleans for many generations and will hopefully continue to do so for many more.

* * *

While the po'boy is synonymous with New Orleans, the sandwich's popularity within the city has helped it make an appearance in multiple other locations outside of the Big Easy. Restaurants that sell what they call "po'boys" can now be found in such far-flung places as St. Louis, Missouri (at Broadway Oyster Bar); Durban, South Africa (at Po'Boys Durban); and even Athens, Greece (at PO'BOYS BBQ). One po'boy shop that has been around for quite a long time, while also showing how po'boys have spread out in areas outside of New Orleans, is **Short Stop Poboys**.

Located at 119 Transcontinental Drive, Short Stop Poboys has been serving the citizens of Metairie, which is the largest community in New Orleans's neighboring Jefferson Parish, for over fifty-five years. A unique aspect of Short Stop Poboys is how its history is directly tied to an element that was once very commonplace in early to mid-twentieth-century New Orleans: mom-and-pop corner grocery stores.

Before the widespread distribution of supermarkets, mom-and-pop grocery stores served as a way for residents in NOLA's neighborhoods to gather food, produce, and more for their homes each week.

A lot of these stores were called "corner grocery stores" because many of them were literally located on the corner of two intersecting streets and even had their entrances directly pointing at said corner. Russell Hendrick, president and owner of Short Stop Poboys, remembers some of the Metairie grocery stores that were near where Short Stop Poboys is now when he was growing up.

"When I was young, just from this location right here, there were four mom-and-pop grocery stores in this neighborhood within four square blocks of here, which is incredible, if you think about it, and each one of them made a living through the people in the neighborhood," Hendrick explains.

According to Hendrick, Short Stop Poboys was originally founded as Short Stop Superette in 1966 by his father, who had experience with small grocery stores in his line of work.

"My dad was a traveling food broker and he covered most of South Louisiana," Hendrick says. "So he would go to all kinds of little grocery stores and supermarkets, which there were a lot of back then because there were a lot of mom-and-pop grocery stores."

Hendrick's father ended up purchasing the building where Short Stop Poboys is now, which was another grocery store, named Jimmy's, and renamed it "Short Stop Superette" to show that it was a "quick stop" grocery store with a variety of goods.

"It had a little bit of everything, fresh meats, fresh produce, in a little bitty place," Hendrick explains. "Everything you wanted, everything you needed, was right there. It was a lot of work, but it was fun. It was life."

According to Hendrick, while the original grocery store did sell po'boys along with meats and produce, the eventual switch over to Short Stop Poboys did not happen until a while after the store opened. Hendrick says his family noticed workers from businesses near Short Stop, the Candle Light Inn and the Garden of Memories Cemetery, would come into the store just to buy supplies to make their own po'boys.

"They had workers at both of those that would come over here every day at lunchtime and buy a little shorty French bread," Hendrick details. "It used to be about eight or nine inches long. One of them would buy a jar of mayonnaise and one of them would buy a head of lettuce and a tomato, and they'd buy twenty-five cents' worth of luncheon meat, salami, or bologna. They'd go outside and make their own sandwiches . . . my parents got the brilliant idea, 'Wait a minute. Why don't we start putting mayonnaise on the sandwich for them and charge them a little bit extra?' Well one thing led to another, 'Why don't we just put meat on the sandwich and charge them for it?'"

Hendrick says another reason the store started serving more po'boys was because the meat did not move fast all the time, so putting it on those sandwiches was an easy way to not have a backed-up inventory. One of the first po'boys that helped get Short Stop Poboys started was roast beef prepared in a slow cooker, and that po'boy continues to be one of the restaurant's most popular sandwiches. Eventually, po'boys just over took the Hendrick family's entire business.

"We started getting less into groceries and more into po'boys," Hendrick says.

With over fifty-five years of serving the Metairie community, Short Stop Poboys has a menu that, according to Hendrick, stays simple and traditional, like what people would make for themselves at home. The shop mostly sees a lot of blue-collar workers who only have a half hour for lunch, so the shop, echoing its name, keeps the po'boys simple so people only have to take a "short stop," whether they are walking into the shop or using the restaurant's drive-up window, to get their sandwiches.

"We keep everything traditional and low-key," Hendrick says. In addition to shrimp, oyster, and roast beef po'boys, the restaurant also has an assortment of cold-cut po'boys such as sliced ham, salami, bologna, luncheon meat, and even liver cheese. According to Hendrick, the shop's liver cheese po'boy has actually been a pretty popular sell. When the entire country was in the midst of the COVID-19 pandemic and shortages on certain items occurred, the shop attracted quite a few people because of that sandwich.

"When we had liver cheese, that's what they came for," Hendrick says. "'You're the only people we could find with liver cheese. We can't find it anywhere, not even in the supermarkets.' People were buying it by the pound."

In another call back to the old family-style grocery stores, Short Stop Poboys is set up exactly like how people would shop, or "make groceries" in Yat, back in the day. Before stores and supermarkets had aisles upon aisles of goods for people to walk through, people would order what they wanted at a counter and then go to a separate line to pay for what they were just given.

"That's the way we work here," Hendrick explains. "You order your food, you get your food, and you carry it to the register and pay. Our style is still like a grocery store."

Despite only being president of Short Stop Poboys for around ten years, Hendrick has been involved with the establishment since his younger days in the 1960s when it was his parents' grocery store. He has also seen how the neighborhood around the shop has changed over the years. In addition to the Candle Light Inn going out of business and the Garden of Memories Cemetery replacing their workers with more machinery for burials, he's also seen a lot of mom-and-pop stores disappear. The only real indication that some residential homes and other businesses, both inside and near NOLA, used to be grocery stores is that the layouts of some of the buildings still retain the corner entrances that were staples of those old shops. One positive change Hendrick has observed is that the road where Short Stop Poboys is located, Transcontinental Drive, has gotten more and more developed, going from a shell-lined road to a fairly busy thoroughfare.

"Transcontinental got to be bigger . . . not as big as Clearview, but it's a big thoroughfare, which is also helpful," Hendrick says. "The more traffic, the more visibility. So things got better and better."

When Hurricane Katrina went through Louisiana in 2005, Metairie made it out of the storm with far less damage than New Orleans did. According to Hendrick, while there was a big loss of food, Short Stop Poboys actually suffered no damage to its building and was closed for just a month.

"It took me about two weeks before I could go back in, locate some employees, start cleaning, and then locate business vendors to try and get food back in, but we recovered very quickly," Hendrick says. "I remember the first day we were opening, I was putting up a sign outside on the building. I was standing on the roof of the building, hanging the open sign, and the parking lot filled up. That was amazing."

Hendrick says while constantly dealing with major hurricanes like Katrina gets old, he has been fortunate to be able to keep his business going and have Short Stop Poboys still be serving the Metairie community for more than half a century.

"It's where we are and it's our foundation," Hendrick says. "Our roots. So many family members lived here and went through the same thing. It's just like, 'They did it. We can do it.'"

In regard to how po'boys have been spreading and becoming more recognizable in the country, Hendrick says he wants to feel like wherever there is a place selling NOLA cuisine outside of Louisiana, it's run by someone who actually left New Orleans for whatever reason. He also says he hopes the NOLA-centric restaurants that are outside the state are actually using real New Orleans French bread, or at least an equivalent, to make what they're serving a truly authentic po'boy.

"My wife watches the food channels all the time and there's a po'boy shop in Vegas," Hendrick says. "Not on the main strip, but off the side. And I actually think that they get their bread from Leidenheimer."

With its overall layout and traditional feel, Short Stop Poboys provides an intriguing little glimpse into the old family-run grocery stores that used to permeate New Orleans, while also showing that there is a strong market for the more classic, home-style po'boys both within and outside of NOLA.

\* \* \*

Another aspect of po'boys, which was cemented when Bennie and Clovis Martin first reached out to the striking streetcar workers of Division 194 in 1929, is the notion that the sandwiches were filling a need within a segment of the New Orleans community. The Martin brothers were literally feeding po'boys to "poor boys," those who suddenly found themselves without a primary source of income and were struggling to survive. This notion to help others is ingrained in the history and ideals of **Melba's**.

Located at 1525 Elysian Fields Avenue, Melba's was founded by husband-and-wife team Scott and Jane Wolfe, who both have a lot of experience with providing necessary services to New Orleans residents. According to Jane Wolfe, she and her husband were in NOLA's grocery business for thirty-five years when they used to work at, own, and operate a number of neighborhood grocery stores, the best-known being Wagner's Meat. That amount of experience proved to be invaluable when they decided to open Melba's, which has an origin story that is directly tied to when Hurricane Katrina swept through the city.

"After Katrina hit, we got into the construction business," Wolfe, who is also Melba's co-owner, explains. "We fixed a couple thousand roofs in New Orleans because all of our groceries were completely inundated with water. You just pivot and try to figure out how to survive, so we had to survive by doing roofs in New Orleans. In two years after doing roofs and doing construction, I had decided to go to school. I went to college for the first time in my life at forty-three years old."

According to a book about the Wolfe family and Melba's called *Melba's Po'boys—A Story Cookbook: America's Busiest Po'boy Shop,* the college that Wolfe went to was Tulane University, and then Harvard Divinity School. While she was away for her studies, her husband actually found a blighted establishment on the intersection of Elysian Fields and North Claiborne avenues, right at the crossroads of New Orleans's Seventh, Eighth, and Ninth wards, all of which suffered heavy damage during Hurricane Katrina.

"It was empty," Wolfe says. "It had nothing in it. He passed this location, and he said, 'What do you think about opening something here?' So while I was in school, I said, 'Yes.'"

With the decision made, the Wolfes started contacting people who used to work with them at Wagner's Meat, including Melba's head chef, "Mama" Lois Thomas, who worked as a cook at Wagner's for about fifteen years. Despite all former employees being dispersed because of Katrina, the Wolfes were able to get familiar faces back together to help turn that damaged structure into something new. That building would ultimately be turned into Melba's on August 2014.

According to Wolfe, Melba's first started as a coffee shop because her husband initially wanted an establishment that was easy to run. However, once they started serving po'boys, people began to congregate there in large numbers. In addition to people looking for a place to gather after Katrina, Melba's location on the intersection of two very busy thoroughfares, as well as its proximity to the French Quarter, also helped because thousands of cars pass by the shop every single day. "This place became a place where everybody that knew one another could gather, and they gathered over po'boys," Wolfe says.

According to Wolfe, po'boys have been in her and husband's blood since their years running Wagner's Meat. All of their grocery stores contained a little deli, located on the side of a forty-foot meat case, that would serve customers freshly made gumbo, jambalaya, baked macaroni, and po'boys. "It's a New Orleans staple," Wolfe says. "We've always served po'boys in our grocery stores."

Melba's menu, which has a home-cooked feel to it, is a hearty mix of full-sized dinners, fried chicken options, and Crescent City classics like red beans, gumbo, and jambalaya. However, the restaurant is particularly known by locals for its wide assortment of po'boys. In addition to a selection of classic po'boys like fried shrimp, roast beef, and French fry, Melba's also offers a number of breakfast po'boys such as bacon, ham, and turkey, all with scrambled eggs, from 4 to 11 a.m. every single day. According to Wolfe, there is one po'boy that is a particular favorite among her customers.

"Our best seller is the hot sausage po'boy," Wolfe says. "We always sold hot sausage po'boys in the grocery store and it's always Patton's hot sausage." In fact, according to Wolfe, she and her husband used to split a hot sausage po'boy almost every day when they were working in the grocery business. "If somebody walks in and asks me what they should get, I tell 'em a hot sausage po'boy," Wolfe says.

In addition to personally liking the simplicity of classic po'boys, which is echoed in the sandwich options that are showcased on Melba's menu, Wolfe believes that Melba's reflects what she considers to be the po'boy's "true essence." That essence, according to Wolfe, directly ties back to when the Martin brothers gave away free sandwiches to the striking streetcar workers in 1929, which involved satisfying a need for people who could not afford to feed themselves.

"The essence of a po'boy has to do with the Martin brothers making a decision to help somebody in need," Wolfe explains. "I believe the Martin brothers were one of the first people in New Orleans to do something that is, in academics today, called 'corporate social responsibility,' which means a business should look at the needs of the community and help its needs. And I think Melba's Po'boy Shop is doing the po'boy justice in regards to what the essence of a po'boy is about."

With years upon years of experience having multiple grocery stores throughout New Orleans's inner-city markets, Wolfe believes that she and the entire Melba's team know the local community's needs, and they strive to address them, along with serving folks authentic NOLA comfort food. "Our po'boy shop is tied to the community because when you walk in, you can feel it and you can see it," Wolfe says.

In addition to mostly employing people who live in the surrounding Eighth and Ninth wards, according to *Melba's Po'boys,* Melba's also has a multitude of washers and dryers inside the restaurant for people needing to do their laundry while getting their food.

"We were in the laundromat business over the thirty-five years of being in business for ourselves," Wolfe says. "We had three laundromats. It was attached to our grocery stores. This is the first time we attached a laundromat to a restaurant. Now would a laundromat in a restaurant work everywhere? No. You got to be good at knowing your community's needs."

Another way Melba's tailors itself toward the community is by being open twenty-four hours a day, seven days a week. Both Wolfe and her husband, with experience in not only the grocery business, but also meat markets, delis, gas stations, and laundromats, know that people always need a certain type of service no matter what time of the day it is, especially in New Orleans, which Wolfe considers to be on the same twenty-four-hour mindset as a certain other "City That Never Sleeps."

"New Orleans is a twenty-four-hour town in the same way that New York is," Wolfe explains. "In the founding of America, New York and New Orleans were port cities. The ports fed this country. New York and New Orleans fed the growth of this country."

With New Orleans's status as not only a major port, but also as one of the major tourism hubs of the United States, there are people in the city who either have to work extended hours or during times when most others are asleep. Having developed a twenty-four-hour mentality from their years with Wagner's Meat and their other community-based services, the Wolfes made a conscious decision to keep Melba's open to feed the people who work at all hours of the day to keep New Orleans's tourism industry functioning. According to Wolfe, before the COVID-19 pandemic, the busiest time for the restaurant was between 10 p.m. and 3 a.m.

"So that's why we're open twenty-four hours," Wolfe says. "Not because we want to get the most business. It's because it's providing a need to a town that initially is set up as a twenty-four-hour town from the days of the port."

But perhaps the greatest example of Melba's drive to capture the spirit of community service with the help of food is the shop's encouragement of literacy. According to Wolfe, Melba's is located in what is considered a "book desert," meaning that most books are hard to come by in that area and residents would have to travel out of the community in order to find printed books. Inspired by her time at college, Wolfe has made Melba's commitment to helping its community members develop a habit to read more just as much a priority as providing good food to eat. Right by the front counter where people go to place their orders, there is a large glass case filled with all kinds of books that Melba's offers to its customers, as well as signs all over informing visitors that they get free food or a free daiquiri if they purchase a book.

"When you come in and you buy a book, you get free food," Wolfe says. "So our po'boy shop, I believe, is tied to the essence of what a po'boy is."

In addition, Wolfe has established a way for published authors to connect with the local community and directly contribute to combating low literacy issues through the Eat & Read at Melba's Literacy Project. According to Melba's website, the program allows authors to participate in a special book signing at Melba's while also giving away one hundred free copies of their books to locals as a way of giving back. Since its inception in 2019, the program has attracted over one hundred authors to take part in it, including New Orleans personalities like former New Orleans mayor Marc Morial, former WWL-TV news anchor Sheba Turk, and Mardi Gras historian Arthur Hardy, as well as internationally known figures like Sister Joan Chittister, Matthew McConaughey, and Hillary and Chelsea Clinton.

"When you come into this po'boy shop, we are addressing literacy and giving people free books," Wolfe says. "This isn't just me throwing free books into the world. The authors participate in handing the free book to people in an area of town that has a societal ill of low literacy."

Not only that, but Melba's also has a program in place that involves giving children free cake and parents free po'boys when the kids come to the restaurant and present an "A" on their most recent report cards. According to Wolfe, the program serves as a celebration for both the children's, as well as the parents', accomplishments.

With a deep passion for serving community-literary opportunities, and po'boys that harken back to the time when the Martin brothers also helped needy locals, all on a twenty-four-hour basis, it's no wonder why Melba's is both so busy and so popular with New Orleanians.

\* \* \*

To survive for over three hundred years, a place has to be willing to adapt. New Orleans is a city that holds firm to its unique traditions, while also pushing forward and evolving into the future, especially when it comes to its food. If the sentiment "a po'boy can contain anything as long as it is held together with French bread" is true, then there are many instances where different establishments have been experimenting with what can be done with a po'boy. Locals and tourists can now find interesting creations like a BBQ shrimp po'boy at Liuzza's by the Track in Mid-City, a "garbage fry" po'boy with cheese, debris, onions, jalapeños, and mushrooms at Rivershack Tavern in Jefferson, and even jerk shrimp, chicken, and fish po'boys at Island Paradise Restaurant & Grill in Gretna.

One of the restaurants representing the ever-changing and ever-evolving side of po'boys is **Killer PoBoys**, which opened in 2012 in the back of Erin Rose, an Irish pub located in the French Quarter that is known best by locals and tourists for its unique frozen Irish coffee. According to Eric Baucom, chef, owner, and operator of Killer PoBoys, the establishment actually started in Erin Rose's small kitchen rent-free just to see if it could make it there.

"We were successful enough down there that, after three years, we bought a second standalone location to where we could expand the menu a little bit and really spread our wings," Baucom says.

The second location is at 219 Dauphine Street, which is about a block and a half from the city's famous major thoroughfare Canal Street. What helps Killer PoBoys draw in customers is that its menu is filled with nothing but po'boys that are exclusive to the shop. According to Baucom, the mission statement that he commits himself to for Killer PoBoys is to provide unique internationally inspired and chef-crafted po'boys to his customers.

"Every po'boy shop in town has their own specialty po'boy that you're not going to find anywhere else," Baucom says. "Here, we just do a whole menu of just nothing but specialty po'boys."

Baucom, who says he has had a career in cooking in high-end hotels, developed his ideas for Killer PoBoys, as well as his mindset about Louisiana cuisine, from working under famed local chef John Folse in Restaurant R'evolution, which is an upscale Cajun/Creole restaurant located in the French Quarter's Royal Sonesta New Orleans Hotel. He says he took his old influences from his career in fine dining to create "a complete plate on a bun."

"I've always gravitated towards the sandwich," Baucom says. "I found one of the best ways to be creative and work around here is to put yourself in a box first and see what you can do within that box. So our box here is a loaf of French bread and, from there, we can do whatever we want to it."

The restaurant's menu is truly eclectic and does not feature any of the traditional po'boys that even most locals are accustomed to seeing. Some of the po'boys featured on the menu include a glazed pork belly with lime cabbage slaw and garlic aioli, as well as a couple of strictly vegetarian po'boys like roasted sweet potato, roasted cauliflower, spinach salad, and Thai BBQ tofu.

"Our most popular, by far, is our seared shrimp," Baucom explains. "It's done up kinda like a Vietnamese bánh mì with that kinda flavor profile. Another thing that we do here that is pretty popular is like half of our sandwich menu is at least vegetarian, if not vegan. As people's diets are changing and everything, there's been like a lack of a market for vegetarian/vegan po'boys in New Orleans. So we found

Glazed pork-belly po'boy from Killer PoBoys.

that as another opportunity to kind of stretch our creativity and do some new and cool things."

Killer PoBoys even goes a bit different with how it approaches its dressing. Since "dressed" is not a static set of ingredients and any restaurant can decide what additional toppings to put on its po'boys, Killer PoBoys has decided to personalize its dressings depending on the particular po'boy that is ordered.

"In the traditional world, 'dressed' could mean a lot of different things . . . everybody's got their own kind of thing," Baucom says. "Over here, we tailor what dressed is to each individual sandwich. Like on our seared shrimp po'boy, you'll have pickled carrots, daikon radish, and cucumber with a sriracha sauce and fresh herbs. Our beef debris will have pickled green beans and banana peppers."

According to Baucom, the French bread, more than the filling, is the most important part of the po'boy. Just like a painting without its canvas, the po'boy would not be a po'boy without its French bread. Baucom says Killer PoBoys actually uses two different types of bread so that the restaurant's various sandwiches can be paired with a specific loaf.

"If I had my way, I'd probably order my bread from five or six different bakeries to better match up the sandwich with the bread that would be best for it," Baucom says. "Unfortunately, that's just not feasible when you're busy. We still use two different types of bread here, but I'd use way more."

Baucom says his main inspiration for the different flavors featured on the Killer PoBoys menu, which range from Asian to Mexican and more, comes from what he's experienced on his travels, bringing tastes from outside of New Orleans and presenting them in a uniquely NOLA way.

"We pull influences from everywhere," Baucom says. "Something that I've eaten somewhere else, something that I've eaten on my travels, I'm going to pull it all back in. The goal is just to make something really, really good that people enjoy eating. We're not scared to pull from anything to make that happen."

According to Baucom, while New Orleans has a great amount of respect for tradition, especially in regard to its food, the city will also continue to move forward and try to add new things to its established customs.

"There's so much room for new twists and new things," Baucom explains. "Here in New Orleans, this food has never been like a 'static thing' and nothing ever goes out of fashion. You just keep layering new stuff on top of it and new stuff on top of it. So po'boys are never going to go out of style, but I think as we go into the future, there's going to be more and more different styles of po'boys and sandwiches like what I'm doing that will eventually become part of the New Orleans tradition once we've been doing it for long enough."

With the notion that anything can be a po'boy as long as it is held together with the iconic French bread, po'boys are perhaps one of NOLA's greatest dishes to showcase how the city's classic cuisine will continue to evolve and adapt for the future, all while staying true to its roots as a sandwich that everyone can enjoy.

"It's always been evolving," Baucom says. "What we try to do is, while maintaining a certain amount of respect for the past, we want to move this whole thing forward. We don't want New Orleans cuisine to turn into a museum. We want to keep going forward with it and keep doing cool and fun things and expand the scope of what people believe a po'boy can be."

Despite opening a couple of years after Hurricane Katrina struck the city, Killer PoBoys still faced some hardships in the early 2020s with the COVID-19 pandemic and Hurricane Ida, both of which caused a good bit of strain on NOLA's restaurant scene. According to Baucom, while Ida caused Killer PoBoys to slow down for about a month, COVID was a more serious ordeal for the restaurant. However, during the pandemic, the po'boy shop was also given a chance to show its resilience, as well as help a community that was also struggling during the pandemic, much like the Martin brothers helped their community back in 1929.

"We were forced, like a lot of other restaurants, to temporarily close our doors for a little while, and an opportunity came our way to partner up with World Central Kitchen," Baucom details. "They partnered us up with a church over in Algiers, which was really cool cause it was really close to my house and I knew some of the people who were members of that church. So we were able to bring some people back to work and start providing meals for people in need rather than open our doors to sell sandwiches to everybody. That kinda got us through a really hard time for a lot of restaurants and I credit that as a big part of why we're able to be open today."

With one foot in the past and another in the future, Killer PoBoys helps show that, no matter what the sandwich is filled with, a po'boy is still a po'boy as long as local French bread is used. Time changes all, and while respect for past traditions is really needed in a city like New

Orleans, evolution and experimentation help prepare the Crescent City for anything that may come in the future. The Big Easy is where the good times roll, and good times are certainly had with po'boys, no matter what they are filled with.

French cold-cut bánh mì from Dong Phuong.

# 5

# The Vietnamese Po'Boy
## *Embracing a New, Yet Familiar, Culture*

In addition to New Orleans's incredible food and beautiful architecture, the Big Easy's citizens are what help it to be one of the most unforgettable cities in the world. If not for the many different ethnic groups that have all developed a notable presence there, New Orleans would not have a unique culture that highlights elements of each group and incorporates their traditions into its own. From the Chitimacha people who first inhabited the lands to the French, Africans, Spanish, and Americans who developed the city, as well as the major migrations of Sicilians, Irish, Germans, Latinos, and others into the city, New Orleans has had more than thirty decades to mix the best aspects of different cultures into its own "gumbo pot."

Some of the Crescent City's relatively newer residents are Vietnamese Americans, who arrived in Greater New Orleans in the mid-1970s. According to "New Orleans Vietnamese Culture" on NewOrleans.com, NOLA's Vietnamese community is at least fourteen thousand strong. While their population size is relatively minuscule when compared to that of larger states like Texas and California, they are one of the largest Asian American demographics in Louisiana. Their presence in New Orleans is largely felt through the numerous Vietnamese restaurants, as well as bakeries, grocery stores, and multiple other businesses owned by Vietnamese families or individuals, scattered within and outside of Orleans Parish. In fact, Mary Queen of Vietnam Church, which is located in the city's New Orleans East area, holds an annual Tết, or Vietnamese New Year, festival that regularly draws large amounts of people to it every year.

There's a strong possibility that, when most Americans hear the word "Vietnam," the only images that might flash into their minds are scenes of war and violence. While parts of Vietnam's history, especially during the twentieth century, have centered on warfare, it's not the sole defining attribute of that country. Vietnam's history dates back thousands of years, and Vietnamese culture is a truly vibrant and interesting mix of both East and Southeast Asia.

One of the best ways to experience another group's culture and history is through their cuisine. Luckily, it is very easy to win over the hearts of many New Orleanians when they're presented with really good food. Since settling into its new home, NOLA's Vietnamese community has made other locals intimately familiar with traditional dishes such as phở (a noodle soup filled with herbs and usually either sliced beef or chicken), bún (a cold vermicelli noodle salad), and, perhaps best of all, bánh mì.

"That's definitely one of my favorites 'cause I see what I see every single day . . . I mean just the crispness and the hot sauce they put on it," Parkway Bakery & Tavern's general manager Justin Kennedy says. "It's just a whole different twist. Talk about reinventing something. They're dynamite."

A staple food of Vietnamese cuisine, a bánh mì is a type of sandwich that uses French-style baguette bread and literally means "bread" in Vietnamese, according to the president of Dong Phuong Baking Company, Linh Tran Garza. The bánh mì actually sounds a bit like a certain beloved Crescent City sandwich.

"A bánh mì is a street food," Garza says. "Even in Vietnam, it's considered a street food. It's very inexpensive. It's on a French bread, a baguette, that came from when Vietnam was a French colony . . . the baguette, even in Vietnam, you don't split it in half kind of like a traditional sandwich, hoagie, or anything else that you see. It's more of a hinge."

The similarities between the bánh mì and NOLA's favorite sandwich are unmistakable. In fact, it is common for bánh mìs to be referred to as "Vietnamese po'boys" in New Orleans.

"I think it's very appropriate," Garza says. "Of course, po'boys are meant to be a type of street food. It's a 'poor boy,' right? It's supposed to be cheap. I think we fit right into that category. I appreciate it."

According to Garza, the flour that is used for the bánh mì bread is a little different from traditional New Orleans French bread, which actually gives the bánh mì a distinctive texture. While retaining the same crispy crust, the bánh mì's interior is slightly different and a little denser. The bread actually lends itself well to being dipped into soups, stews, and curries and is good at absorbing a good amount of broth.

"Other po'boy breads, they use a higher protein content flour," Garza explains. "So the po'boy bread is not as dense on the inside. The bánh mì bread has a very thin crust that's crispy on the outside, but the inside has a consistency of almost like white bread."

In addition, while po'boys can have a huge variety of completely different fillings and toppings, bánh mìs tend to have a few ingredients that are almost always needed to properly identify them as bánh mìs.

"Traditionally, it has a mayonnaise or aioli," Garza details. "It's made from egg yolks, so it has that yellow color. In Vietnamese, we call it 'bơ,' which directly translates to 'butter,' but it doesn't have any butter. It's just 'cause it's yellow, so it looks like butter, but it's mostly just egg yolks and oil. And the other traditional spread that goes with it is a pâté. It's made usually from either pork liver, chicken liver, or a combination of that."

According to Garza, fillings such as meatballs, grilled pork, Vietnamese ham (which is sort of like bologna), and other meats that can be typically found on rice plates have been used for bánh mìs throughout the years.

"Also from French influences is this other pork, we call it a 'French-style ham,' where it's an equivalent of like a head cheese 'cause there's pork skin," Garza says.

According to Garza, her favorite type of bánh mì is more on the traditional side: French-style cold cuts with lots of pâté and lots of aioli. Toppings that are commonly seen on the sandwich include cucumbers, cilantro, jalapeños, pickled carrots, and daikon. Additionally, bánh mìs can be eaten at any time of the day, and it is not uncommon to see bánh mì stands and phở places in Vietnam serving food very early in the morning. According to Garza, Vietnamese meals look a bit different from what average Americans are used to seeing.

"I think about a Vietnamese dinner and traditionally, even in my own household with my family and everything, it's more dishes," Garza explains. "Typically, these single types of dishes like a bowl of phở or bánh mì are breakfast and lunch, but when you sit down for dinner, you have a stir-fry, you have a soup, you have a meat dish. When my mom made dinner growing up, it was hardly ever one dish. It's a spread."

So while there are some noticeable differences between a bánh mì and a po'boy, the similarities between the two are so close that it's no surprise that the "Vietnamese po'boy" nickname has stuck in New Orleans. In fact, these two sandwiches can actually serve as an important visual link between New Orleans and Vietnam, which share quite a few parallels, such as a humid climate and direct access to large bodies of water (the Mississippi River for New Orleans and the South China Sea and Mekong Delta for Vietnam).

The biggest shared aspect between New Orleans and Vietnam is a history of being French colonies, although Vietnam saw a lot more violence in its road towards decolonization than New Orleans ever did. France's major involvement within Vietnam started in the eighteenth century, when it started trading with and providing military assistance to the soon-to-be ruling Nguyễn dynasty. France then launched a series of military operations, with the help of Spain, against the Nguyễn dynasty from 1858 to 1862 in what is now called the Cochinchina Campaign, which ended with France gaining major militaristic and economic dominance within the region and establishing French Cochinchina in what is now southern Vietnam. After that, France expanded out to establish territories in what is now northern Vietnam, Cambodia, Laos, and a small section of China, thus officially forming French Indochina in Southeast Asia.

With Vietnam firmly under its control, France worked to boost its influence and leave its mark on the country, which would ultimately lead to Vietnam being forever changed. The French language was given sole official status in the territories, French colonial buildings were being erected in major cities like Saigon and Hanoi, the Vietnamese language was changed from its historical Chinese character-based script to a Latin-based one, people were getting converted from their folk religions to Catholicism, and French cuisine was being introduced to the locals. Baguettes in particular started to be either incorporated into existing dishes or transformed into new ones by the local inhabitants.

France's grip on the region started to loosen during World War II when Nazi Germany knocked the country out of the war in 1940 and established the puppet Vichy government, as well as when Imperial Japanese forces invaded parts of the region that same year to spread Japan's empire into Southeast Asia. Not only that, Vietnamese independence groups, most notably the communist united-front group called the Viet Minh (led by a certain someone named Hồ Chí Minh), were forming to resist foreign occupation. Hồ Chí Minh even officially declared Vietnam's independence in September 1945 during the August Revolution. France then fought against the Viet Minh from 1945 to 1946 in what is called "the War in Vietnam," which then led into the

First Indochina War from 1946 to 1954. That war finally ended with France completely pulling out of Vietnam and the country being split in half as a result of the 1954 Geneva Conference, with North Vietnam being pro-communist and South Vietnam being anti-communist. Just one year later would be the official start of what has become known in the United States as the Vietnam War.

Now that is a bit of heavy geopolitical backstory for a book about po'boys, but it's important to know where Vietnam was at that time in its history and how this separation caused the bánh mì to eventually make its way to the Crescent City. The Vietnam War was a very complicated period of history that forever changed both Vietnam and the United States, so an analysis of the decisions that were made during the war is not within the scope of this book. The thing to take away from that conflict is that it cost the lives of millions upon millions of people and forced just as many to become refugees and forever leave their homeland for America. Almost every single Vietnamese American family has a story of survival it its history, and this includes Garza's family, especially her parents, Huong and De Tran.

"They grew up in a village in Vietnam, in the south, about six hours from Saigon," Garza details. "My mom's dad had a bakery and a café/noodle shop. She grew up there. With her dad having a business, she was a little bit more well off than my dad growing up. I wouldn't say she was rich or anything, but maybe middle class if I had to put her."

Garza says that, while her mother, Huong, helped out a little bit in her grandfather's bakery, her mom told her it was never her dream.

"She went to Saigon for college, but she was only able to finish one year—not even a year—because the war came south," Garza says. "There was so much fear about the bombings and everything, so her dad made her come home. She wasn't able to finish, but her dream was to work in a bank."

Garza says, even though that was her mother's dream, she was still able to kind of help out around the family bakery and gain some working experience.

"She was able to kind of see how things were working, even though she didn't really get her hands 'dirty' in a sense," Garza says. "I think that helped when she came over here and helped with all of the recipes."

Garza's dad, De, did more agrarian work and had plots of land that he would tend to at his home.

"He was always really smart," Garza says. "He also went to school. I think he was studying agriculture, but, of course, he was drafted when he was of age. He was selected to be in the Air Force, but only for maybe a year or two before the Fall [of Saigon]. Thankfully he survived, which you can't say for many others."

Huong and De ended up getting married sometime after the Fall of Saigon and were living together on De's farm when Garza was born in 1978. According to Garza, when communist forces took over Vietnam, they shuttered businesses and shuffled people who had been loyal to South Vietnam, as well as prevented people from certain business establishments from going to school.

"They didn't let businesses stay open," Garza says. "They took all of the money in the banks. So it was a very hard time."

According to Garza, her family struggled to find any opportunities to support themselves. Not only did her grandfather's bakery business end up closing down, the family was blocked from job opportunities because of her dad's military affiliation with South Vietnam.

"I think that's when they decided that in order to provide their children with opportunities, they would need to leave," Garza explains. "So after multiple tries, we were able to board some sort of boat, from what my mom described, with hundreds of others. I was six months old at the time when we left, so I was pretty young. And I think that's why I don't like boats. You know, repressive memory . . . we landed in Malaysia, and we were there for maybe about a year in the refugee camp. I mean, it was an arduous journey."

Apparently, according to stories that her mother told her, the ship that Garza's family was traveling on, which included herself, her parents, her older brother, and her dad's family, was stopped and raided by pirates.

"They took everything," Garza says. "It was just scary."

While staying in Malaysia, Garza's family applied around to different countries before they were given a chance to come to America.

"I think my dad wanted to go to Australia because he wanted to continue with his agriculture," Garza says. "But since he was in the Air Force, he was fighting for the non-communist side, he had priority with the U.S. So we're like, 'Ok!' He had a friend who was in the Armed Forces with him, but left in '75 after the Fall [of Saigon] . . . I guess he was flown out with the other troops. He settled in New Orleans and he was able to sponsor us."

In addition to similar climates and shared French colonial roots, a lot of Vietnamese refugees were Catholic, according to NewOrleans.com's "New Orleans Vietnamese Culture," so Catholic charities also had a hand in sponsoring families and helping them to settle within Greater New Orleans. One of areas where many Vietnamese families ended up congregating in was the Village de L'Est neighborhood of New Orleans East, which is where Garza grew up with nine other family members in a rental shotgun house. According to her, the newly formed Vietnamese community in Village de L'Est helped each other in the resettling process, showed each other where to go to get supplies and groceries, and also assisted each other with learning English.

"I think everybody felt comfortable here," Garza says. "If you settled here, the Vietnamese community helped to take you in."

Because her mom was not able to finish college and could not speak English, she had no prominent "marketable skills" and could not follow her banking dream in her new home, according to Garza. So in order to support her soon to be three children (with Garza's younger sister being born in New Orleans), Huong decided to fall back on the knowledge and skills she gathered from her dad's bakery. In fact, she would send letters to her parents, who stayed behind in Vietnam, and ask them to send her their recipes for pastries in a process that took many months since this was before email was in widespread use.

"She would start making the cakes that she grew up with from her father's bakery," Garza explains. "Just different pastries. She would take them to the local grocery stores down the street and, you know, it was selling well. So everything just sort of picked up from there."

While Garza's mother was supporting the family by selling her baked goods, other family members were also pitching in by working at one of the first Vietnamese restaurants in New Orleans. It was called Dong Phuong Restaurant, located on 14207 Chef Menteur Highway, which is where the current Dong Phuong Bakery & Restaurant is located. Before Dong Phuong came under the ownership of Garza's family, it was run by a family that was looking to move to Baton Rouge and sell the establishment.

"My grandmother, my uncle, and my aunt, they were all working in that restaurant for the owner," Garza says. "So when the owner was gonna sell and they were gonna leave, my grandmother was like, 'We can do this if we just gather all of our resources.' She said she prayed on it and then she was like, 'I think this could work.' We just all pitched in and they got the restaurant. So my dad started the bakery using the restaurant's kitchen in the back and it just started to kinda expand from there."

Dong Phuong Bakery officially opened in 1982 and at first specialized in traditional Vietnamese pastries such as bean cakes and mooncakes, which have a crispy crust and a paste-like filling. Despite shipping their baked goods to multiple Asian grocery stores in other states, the bakery stayed relatively unknown outside of the local Vietnamese community. According to Garza, Dong Phuong didn't start serving bánh mìs until about a decade after the bakery was established because Garza's grandfather did not originally serve any bánh mìs in Vietnam. Garza's father was actually the one who got Dong Phuong to start selling the sandwiches after reading many recipes and trying them out for himself.

"He just kept testing, tinkering, using different recipes," Garza says. "Finally, he created a recipe for bánh mìs that he was very happy about and that was probably in the '90s."

Some of the bánh mìs that Dong Phuong offers range from traditional fillings like French cold cuts, Vietnamese ham, and liver pâté to more experimental options like toasted fish patties, rotisserie chicken, and Chinese roast beef. Garza believes that, once Dong Phuong started selling its bánh mì bread and sandwiches, that was when the bakery really started to see larger growth and become a recognizable name in New Orleans, as well as one of the premier Vietnamese bakeries in the entire city.

"It was a crossover product," Garza says. "Everybody in New Orleans knows French bread, right? It's different from a po'boy bread, but it's still bread. So it was a lot easier to cross over into a new demographic, and I think that's when we started really growing faster."

When Hurricane Katrina struck in 2005, most of New Orleans East suffered severe flooding. According to Garza, while Dong Phuong did sustain some damage, it definitely was not enough to shutter the business for good. The bakery and restaurant were shut down for about four months, with an additional amount of time needed to rebuild.

"I think everybody was elated when we did come back," Garza says. "The whole community came back. I think it was a shock to most how fast our community came back, but I think it goes back to the sentiment of, 'We already left. We already fled. We already lost everything before. We didn't want to do that again, to start all over again after having to leave our country behind and everything. We already started this new home, so let's stick it out and stay.'"

Dong Phuong persevered through Katrina and has been continuing to move forward ever since the business was able to open back up again. As acceptance among local New Orleanians for more traditional Vietnamese foods like phở and bún continued to grow, so did the bakery and restaurant's popularity. Dong Phuong's baked goods and bánh mì bread can now be found in many grocery stores and restaurants across Greater New Orleans. The bakery also received acclaim when, in 2008, it started selling its own brand of king cakes, which locals go crazy for every year during the Mardi Gras season. Over thirty years of experience and work culminated in 2018 when Dong Phuong Bakery was named an "American Classic Award" winner by the James Beard Foundation.

"When they sent me an email, I thought it was spam," Garza explains. "I didn't believe it. I was like, 'James Beard? Really?' And it was not until they called and I was like, 'Oh, wow!' And to be recognized as an American classic. A Vietnamese bakery in the outskirts of New Orleans is considered an American classic. It's like, 'Really? Wow!'"

Considering how her family had to leave their original home and come to America with basically nothing, as well as how much time and effort her parents put toward Dong Phuong to make it what it is today, Garza says for the bakery to be officially labeled an American classic was like achieving the American Dream.

"We felt even more proud, I think, when the news reached Vietnam," Garza says. "I think I cried. I shed a tear when family members in Vietnam called and told us, 'Hey, I saw you in the Vietnamese paper over there. You're in the paper over there saying you won an American culinary award, a James Beard Award.' And everybody was just so happy."

Now, locals and visitors alike can find bánh mìs all over Greater New Orleans. They can be found at establishments that cater to a wide range of Vietnamese cuisines like Dong Phuong Bakery & Restaurant, shops that are specifically tailored to bánh mìs like Mr. Bubbles in both New Orleans and Gretna, in Asian supermarkets like Gretna's Hong Kong Food Market, and shops that experiment with specialty fusion bánh mìs like Banh Mi Boys in Uptown New Orleans and Metairie. Garza says that she's always open to trying a different spin on bánh mìs, especially since the sandwich has become more "hipster," in her own words.

"I'm always curious to see how bánh mìs are going to go from here since it's become more well-known . . . With different cultures being in the same vicinity, of course there's going to be different influences," Garza says. "I'd like to see that. I'm not against fusion or anything. I'm just curious how people would take it."

Garza believes a major contributing factor that really helped to make Dong Phuong such a success for so long is New Orleans's welcoming nature. In a city that has such a wide array of different ethnicities and cultures mixing together, it was relatively easy for New Orleanians to accept not only the bakery, but also the Vietnamese community as a whole.

"It is amazing how New Orleans has accepted and still continues to accept new cultures," Garza says. "I wish that more cities can be like us."

Whether it is called a bánh mì or a "Vietnamese po'boy," this different, but familiar, sandwich has absolutely found itself a good home in the Big Easy.

\* \* \*

So how can a sandwich represent an entire city? Quite easily. The po'boy's history shows that New Orleanians will look after each other in times of need. The French bread used for the sandwich shows New Orleans can embrace its roots, while also being willing to change and adapt to its surroundings. All of the different po'boy varieties demonstrate the love NOLA's citizens have for something familiar, as well as their willingness to try something new. The sheer number of restaurants solely dedicated to po'boys, or just featuring a few loaves on their menus, reveals the popularity and longevity of the sandwich among locals and tourists. The presence of "Vietnamese po'boys" shows the city's welcoming nature, as well as its embrace and incorporation of many different people into its own one-of-a-kind culture.

When people come to New Orleans for even a short visit, they leave with memories of a city full of beautiful architecture, music in the air, and great-tasting food. However, if they choose to look deeper or stay longer, they will find so much more. They will find a city with some of the most hospitable and strongest people they will ever meet. People who work hard so they can play harder. People who will greet anyone with a smile and a "How ya doin', baby?" People who would not think twice about inviting someone new to supper and sharing their life stories with them. If southern hospitality really does exist, then it is exemplified in New Orleans. Anyone who comes down to the Big Easy is welcomed with open arms, and everyone who stays long enough becomes family. And like all families, NOLA will always come together around a dinner table loaded with gumbo, red beans, beignets, and humble, historic, traditional, creative, resilient po'boys.

Here comes another survivor. Here comes another new member of the family. Here comes another lover of life and of great-tasting food. Here comes another poor boy.

# Sources and Further Reading

**Personal Interviews**

Eric Baucom, July 6 and 21, 2022.

Joanne and Ken Domilise, June 28 and July 18, 2022.

Linh Tran Garza, June 29, 2022.

Jason Gendusa, July 1 and December 2, 2022.

Russell Hendrick, July 14, 2022.

Justin Kennedy, June 30, 2022.

Sandy Whann, June 27 and December 1, 2022.

Jane Wolfe, July 5, 2022.

**Websites**

"About Po-Boy Fest," poboyfesttickets.com (Oak Street Poboy Fest).

acmeoyster.com (Acme Oyster House).

antoines.com/about#our-history (Antoine's).

beviseafoodco.com.

bindersbakery.com (Binder's Retro).

bmbsandwiches.com.

bontempsboulets.com.

broadwayoysterbar.com/index.html.

casamentosrestaurant.com.

domilisespoboys.com (SCD Marketing).

dpbakery.com.

erinrosebar.com (Erin Rose).

facebook.com/hidobakery.

facebook.com/hkmfnola.

facebook.com/MrBubblesCafe.

frenchmarket.org (French Market Corporation, 2017–23).

gendusabakery.com (Gendusa Bakery).

"German Culture in New Orleans" (NewOrleans.com).

islandparadisenola.com (Island Paradise Restaurant & Grill).

killerpoboys.com.

leidenheimer.com.

lejeunesbakery.com (LeJeune's Bakery).

liuzzasbtt.com.

mahonyspoboys.com (Mahony's Po-Boys & Seafood, 2016–23).

melbas.com.

"New Orleans Vietnamese Culture" (NewOrleans.com).

parkwaypoorboys.com (Michael Mizell-Nelson, "History of the Poor Boy").

poboy.co.za (Po'Boys Durban).

poboysbbq.gr.

rivershacktavern.com.

shortstoppoboysno.com.

Susan Waggoner, "The Po' Boy: New Orleans' Super Star Sandwich" (ForknPlate, 2015).

yeoldecollegeinn.com.

### Printed Sources

Chevallier, Jim. *About the Baguette: Exploring the Origin of a French National Icon.* Self-published, 2014.

Grace, Roger M. "Oysters Stuffed in Toast: Po' Boy, Peacemaker, Oyster Loaf." *Los Angeles Metropolitan News-Enterprise,* May 20, 2004.

Ladies of the St. Francis Street Methodist Episcopal Church, South. *Gulf City Cook Book.* Dayton, OH: United Brethren Publishing House, 1878.

Mizell-Nelson, Michael. "Po-Boy Sandwich." *64 Parishes,* 2013.

*The Picayune Creole Cook Book, 6th ed. 1901; New Orleans:* Times-Picayune Publishing Co., 1922.

Randolph, Mary. *The Virginia House-Wife; Or, Methodical Cook*. 1824; Baltimore, MD: Plaskitt, Fite & Co., 1838.

Wolfe, Scott and Jane. *Melba's Po'boys—A Story Cookbook: America's Busiest Po'boy Shop.* StoryTerrace, 2019.